Praise for *Kindness*

'A reminder that hope and love exist all around us, even when it seems that all is lost. Kath's journey is an inspiration to us all.' ISA GUHA, broadcaster and former England cricketer

'Kath's story is so incredible and compelling in itself, but through this beautiful book she invites and inspires the reader to really contemplate how kindness—in all its attributes—can help us each live our lives more richly.' SARAH HARDEN, CEO of Hello Sunshine

'This book will change your life. Kath Koschel shows us that choosing to deliberately move towards each other in kindness is the antidote to a world that's increasingly frightening.' OSHER GÜNSBERG, television presenter and founder of the *Better Than Yesterday* podcast

'*Kindness* is one of the most powerful and uplifting books I've ever read and had a profound impact on me. It had me teary and smiling at the same time, and it beautifully captures how kindness can be the solution to overcoming adversity and the incredible healing powers of human connection. It also provides a simple twelve-step framework for making kindness our competitive advantage in today's world, which is why everyone needs to read this book.' BEN CROWE, mindset coach and leadership mentor

'Much like Kath herself, *Kindness* is a breath of fresh air. A story of resilience, strength, growth and, of course, kindness. You cannot walk away from Kath or from the story that she has laid bare without feeling deeply touched. A gentle reminder to really live, a warm reminder to be kind and a strong reminder that there is always light at the end of the tunnel.' BRITTANY HOCKLEY, co-founder of the *Life Uncut* podcast

'I picked it up; I could not put it down. What a beautiful book. What a beautiful journey. Kath is the kindest person I know and is a gift to us all.' GUS WORLAND, founder of Gotcha4Life

Kindness.

Kath Koschel

ALLEN&UNWIN
SYDNEY • MELBOURNE • AUCKLAND • LONDON

Allen & Unwin
Cammeraygal Country
83 Alexander Street
Crows Nest NSW 2065
Australia
Phone: (61 2) 8425 0100
Email: info@allenandunwin.com
Web: www.allenandunwin.com

Allen & Unwin acknowledges the Traditional Owners of the Country on which we live and work. We pay our respects to all Aboriginal and Torres Strait Islander Elders, past and present.

 A catalogue record for this book is available from the National Library of Australia

NATIONAL LIBRARY OF AUSTRALIA

ISBN 978 1 76106 883 6

Set in 12.5/19 pt Adobe Caslon Pro by Midland Typesetters, Australia
Printed and bound in Australia by the Opus Group

10 9 8 7 6 5 4 3 2 1

For future generations

Contents

Introduction

In August 2016, I set off on a journey around Australia with nothing but the clothes on my back and my phone—no cash, credit card, food or water. In order to survive, I would have to accept the help and kindness of strangers. I had no idea how long I would last, but I did know that it was going to be either the best or the worst decision of my life.

The original impetus to leave really began four years earlier, when I was in a wheelchair after breaking my back for the first time. I was still in the very early days of the rehabilitation process and you only had to look at me the wrong way and I would burst into tears. I was having an identity crisis. I'd been robbed of my childhood dream of being a professional cricketer, and then one afternoon, during a session with my rehab team, I was told that there was a very high possibility that I also might never walk again. After the session, as I sat in my wheelchair next to the elevator, my emotions close to the surface, I suddenly felt like there wasn't enough air in the corridor. I desperately needed to get downstairs to my room, where I could breathe again without others seeing my tears.

I could never have anticipated that being unable to reach the button to call the elevator would be the thing that pushed me beyond my breaking point. My injuries had limited my movement, and from my wheelchair the button was just out of reach—a matter of centimetres. Despite all the challenges I'd faced in recent weeks—having multiple surgeries, quitting my job and packing up my life for the indefinite future—this was the first time I felt truly broken. It was an emotional fracture that I hadn't experienced before in my twenty-five years on Earth.

I felt completely crushed. And also a little silly and embarrassed. I had always prided myself on my self-reliance, and valued having a sense of control of my life. Not only had I now lost all independence, I had started to fear that this would be what it was like for the rest of my life.

I dropped my head into my hands, hoping no one would see me. Tears streamed from my eyes. The *ping* of the elevator forced me to raise my head, just in time to notice that a man had pressed the down arrow for me, then walked off down the hall.

The man hadn't said anything, and I couldn't muster the energy between my tears to call out a thank you for his simple gesture. But it was a profound moment for me: for perhaps the first time in my life, I felt connected to something bigger than myself.

We hadn't exchanged words—we hadn't even made eye contact—but that man and I had connected through kindness. He was able to give it, and I was able to receive it. I wheeled myself into the lift and made my way to my room.

By the time I got there, the tears that had escaped me only moments before were fading into distant memory. With gritted teeth, I looked at myself in the bathroom mirror and I told myself that I would walk again. If not for myself, then for all the people who had helped me, just as that stranger had.

There was more to his act, I realised, than just pressing a button when he'd seen I wasn't able to. His small gesture told me that *I was not alone*. Somehow it felt like he believed in me, and that I needed to believe in myself again too. Just as he had chosen to help me, I had to choose to help myself.

Perhaps my decision, four years later, to leave my home and embark on my kindness journey was because I was longing to feel this way again. Perhaps I needed a kick-start to remind myself that I could overcome anything, and connecting with others had always inspired me to do so. Or maybe it was an act of kindness to myself. Maybe I was putting on my own oxygen mask before I could help those around me, just like the airline safety drill says.

Even now, I'm still not really sure what made me choose to test out the kindness of strangers in such a risky way. But I am so grateful that I did.

• • •

I don't claim to be an expert in anything, and especially not kindness. This might surprise some people, given I started a global movement called the Kindness Factory and I'm writing a book about it. Sure, I spend most days talking about the benefits and opportunities kindness can bring, and I do my utmost to root all my behaviour in kindness. But it's a lifelong work in progress, and I'm learning all the time.

I think of myself as an accidental motivational speaker. I'd never set out to feature on the speaking circuit, where these days I present to everyone from high-flying corporates and celebrities to schoolchildren and those living rough on the street. When I first accepted an invitation to share my life lessons on stage, I worried that headlining 'kindness' as my subject matter would turn people off—I thought they might roll their eyes, as if they'd heard it all before. I know that kindness can seem sickly-sweet—like surface-level 'niceness'. Dictionaries use words like 'friendly', 'generous' and 'considerate' to describe it. But what do those words really mean on a practical level?

For me, kindness is a set of actions to live by, a manifesto that expresses qualities that we can hold ourselves accountable to. But what if we could think of kindness as a call to action? Or even as a way to live?

The way I see it, kindness underpins every part of our lives: everything we do and everything we should strive to be. As humans evolved, we have learned that kindness is important—maybe the most important thing of all—for any functioning society. But why do I think that kindness trumps everything? And why does doing something for others—performing an act of kindness—feel so inherently *good*?

When I started the Kindness Factory and adopted a mindset of kindness, my life quickly began to make more sense to me. I am someone who has been through their fair share of adversity and learned some valuable lessons along the way. But the more I tried to change my behaviour to be of service to myself and others, the more I realised that practising kindness made me feel good. I began to appreciate the small things in life more, my mood improved and my perspective shifted. I was more resilient, happier and healthier than I had ever been before.

I'm not someone who has ever really struggled with the concepts of compassion, empathy and decency, but when

5

I made kindness an active choice in my everyday life, and when I recognised the power that has, it became something that I could look forward to and be grateful for.

One of the reasons for this, I believe, is that 'kindness' is an umbrella term, incorporating a plethora of other important human qualities. This is why there are so many ways to be kind. To ourselves, to others and to the communities and society we live in. Buying a stranger a coffee is an act of kindness, but so is making a joke that puts a new friend at ease. Unpacking the dishwasher for your household is kindness, but so is smiling at a stranger on the street, or quietly telling someone they've got a popcorn kernel shell stuck in their teeth. Sitting beside someone gravely ill, giving your time or money to a charity or simply listening to someone talk about their problems are all forms of kindness.

In mid-2018, having for two years done more talks in school assembly halls and corporate workplaces than I could count, I realised I needed to do more to help people understand the value of kindness. I was seeing the impact my talks were having on kids and adults, but I was just one person. I couldn't talk to everyone.

After being introduced to Rob Regan, the head of Kaplan Australia, who was inspired by my life story and the vision I had to influence our education system, I began working with a team of academics and researchers to develop a curriculum of kindness. Change starts with our kids, so I wanted to do everything I could to make the next generation the kindest and most resilient people possible. My goal was to produce a set of age-appropriate resources that teachers could use to inspire students to act with kindness and practise better wellbeing strategies.

In March 2020, at the beginning of the first COVID-19 lockdown in Australia, I sat in my apartment in Sydney's Northern Beaches and read hundreds of emails from parents who were finding it difficult to entertain their children during the enforced isolation. Word had got out that we were in the design phase of our curriculum offering, and my details were publicly available online. Teachers were sending schoolwork home and teaching lessons online via Zoom, but most children had finished their schoolwork by midmorning. By now our team of academics and researchers were deep in the process of developing our curriculum, but we were still a long way off launching the finished product.

As the long lockdown went on, more and more parents and teachers reached out. 'Is it ready yet?' their emails would ask, with thinly veiled desperation. I knew we had to get our skates on.

The Kindness Curriculum was launched in 60 schools two months later. Today, just over two years later, that same curriculum has been accessed by over 3000 Australian schools and introduced in the United States and the United Kingdom.

The curriculum is based on the twelve attributes that we believe make kindness what it is: self-acceptance, perspective, humility, gratitude, mindfulness, positivity, collaboration, empathy, trust, humour, honesty and compassion. Our original plan was to get the curriculum resources in front of as many children as possible to inspire a generational change of kindness, but as the pandemic escalated, our priority became to boost kids' wellbeing and encourage resilience at a time when they needed it most.

• • •

I was first approached to write a book about my life story four years ago. I felt very flattered to be asked, but my answer was no. I felt too young to write a book, and I believed that only important people wrote books, not battlers like me! Plus, I thought, my story wasn't over yet—I wasn't finished learning all that I would need to know if I were ever to put pen to paper.

When I was approached again at the end of 2021, I was a little bit older, yet I still felt my story wasn't over—though probably that's how every memoirist feels. But something had changed. This time I felt like I had something important to say, something I could see was urgently needed in the world. I already knew I had something valuable to share from telling my story to thousands of people around the world, but now I also had something that could be put into action— the Kindness Curriculum. We'd targeted schools to effect the generational change we hoped was possible, but in the meantime, I now saw, adults were doing it tough too.

The twelve attributes of kindness we cover in the Kindness Curriculum are common themes in my own life. They reflect my own personal values, but they are also qualities I noticed in others during my years of adversity and challenge.

When I sat down to write my story, I realised that the Kindness Curriculum was much more than just a program to be taught in schools. These twelve concepts underpin everything I know to be good and important in our world. They're my blueprint for happiness. They work together and separately, but they're all part of the DNA of kindness. And they're also the key to making the world a better place.

I've learned about these attributes from the people I've met along my life's journey, and never more so than in the two months I travelled the country with nothing but a change of clothes and a toothbrush. In that time I shared parts of my life with some incredible characters, and I had many unexpected people share parts of their lives with me. That's not to say this book will be all beer and skittles. In parts it's probably not an easy read, because a lot of what I experienced has not been easy to live through.

But my hope is that, the next time you are faced with a choice—whether to act with kindness or turn your back on it—you choose kindness. Not just because it's the right thing to do, but because I know you will never regret that decision. Kindness and everything that we allow it to be is good for those on whom you bestow it, but it's also undeniably very good for you too. It can change your life, and the lives of people you haven't even met yet.

That's what I know as the power of kindness.

The idea

The months leading up to my decision to embark on my journey into the unknown were some of the toughest of my life.

I'd had a hard few years since I made my cricket debut for New South Wales: a debilitating spinal injury, six surgeries on my back, months and months of rehab, and—most painful of all—the death of my partner, Jim. I had learned to walk again, but emotionally I was still limping for quite some time. Eventually, with time and the kindness of both my support network and strangers, I had rediscovered the good in the world and my life was on the up.

Almost eight months before getting on the train to start my journey, I had been hit by a four-wheel drive while on a training bike ride with friends. On that summer morning, my back was broken in four places. And I had spent the four years before that teaching myself how to walk again, and been in and out of hospitals and rehab centres.

People often think I'm joking when I say I've had to teach myself how to walk again twice over as an adult, but the reality of it isn't funny at all. My second recovery process was especially gruelling. It was as if I'd hit rewind on my life and been thrown headfirst back into the trauma of the first recovery.

That second rehab had worn me down. I was constantly reminded of the traumatic time I'd had the first time around, after my first broken back and losing my partner. I wasn't myself anymore, and everyone who cared about me knew it. I was so keen to get out of rehab this time that I tried to speed everything up by doing extras with my physical injuries, completely avoiding the emotional toll that the experience was taking on me.

My best friend Erin, who was with me when I was hit by the car, is herself a physiotherapist, and she sat with me almost every day when I was in the early stages of my recovery. As I regained strength, Erin prescribed me extra exercises, knowing how badly I wanted to walk again.

While I was confident that my physical injuries would heal, I continued to suppress the emotions that were creeping closer to the surface every day. They weren't necessarily from this injury, but from the first time I was a full-time inpatient in rehab, in 2012 following my first broken back playing cricket.

It wasn't all bad, though. Only two months before this most recent accident, I had started a social media page and website called the Kindness Factory, which I saw as a side project— my full-time job was in sport. I'd already been surprised at the rise in popularity of the Kindness Factory, which encouraged people to share acts of kindness. It was a simple idea, but gave me an immediate sense of purpose whenever I was working on it. What had started as a way of me paying forward some of the kindness I had received in my life quickly grew into a movement of people who simply wanted to do good.

When the Kindness Factory community heard of my cycling accident, and while I was still in recovery, I heard from hundreds of people from all around the world who wanted to spur me on in my recovery. Looking back now, I still smile at the goodwill of all of those people who made a pretty dark time in my life a little bit more bearable.

In rehab, I struggled the most at night-time. Mostly it was the silence in the corridors, which gave me too much time to think. So, it was always a welcome distraction to receive messages, emails and social media posts—they helped occupy my mind and fill the silence.

After I was discharged from rehab, I was almost celebrated by the people around me. Work colleagues excitedly came up and hugged me when they saw me back in the office for the first time. My family were stoked to have me back with them—my nephews especially loved the fact that their aunty was back and could play Ninja Turtles again. All I remember feeling, though, was incredibly lost.

Who was I? How on earth had life thrown all this at me? And what did it all mean? I woke up most mornings with a lump in my throat, which I swallowed for most of the day until night-time came and I cried myself to sleep. Enough was enough, I decided—I needed help.

I began talking to a few trusted friends, trying to find myself again. There was Corinne, who always thought I was a little 'out there' but still entertained my ideas. There was Erin, who has *always* had my back, and whom I trust most in this world, and who is also reliable, consistent and sometimes too sensible. And there was Carla, my hype girl.

I remember exactly where I was when I called Carla. I was sitting on the lounge in my apartment, and it was a Wednesday evening about seven months after my accident. I thought I was in a good enough place emotionally to hear her bright tones, but when she answered the phone, the safety of her voice made me burst into tears. I shared with her how lost I was feeling and a lot of what was on my mind.

There's something about Carla that is so warm and beautiful that it immediately makes you feel good—that's why I call her 'Magic'. It doesn't matter what mood you're in, you always feel infinitely better after talking to Carla. She is pure gold, and the embodiment of goodness. I am so lucky to call her a friend.

During what became a two-hour conversation, I mentioned to Carla that I had an idea. It was a bit out there, I said, so she would have to bear with me as I explained it.

'I'm thinking of leaving my home with nothing but the clothes on my back,' I explained. 'No cash or credit cards, and no help from immediate family or friends. I want to see how far I can go. I might last only a few hours, hopefully more than that. It just feels like the right thing to do—I feel like it will get me back on track. What do you think?'

I held my breath as I waited for her response. When she asked me why I believed this was a good idea, I couldn't think of any other explanation than that I just needed to find a little perspective again. I believed in the power of kindness: it had already proved itself to me once, and I somehow knew that I would be afforded that same experience again. I felt this was a logical step towards feeling like myself again.

'Kath, I think you're amazing,' Carla said, 'and if this is what you think will allow you to find yourself again, then you should do it.'

That was all the encouragement I needed to throw myself into the idea.

When we hung up, it was about 10 pm and we had come up with a plan. I would put a post on social media explaining what I was doing. I took a photo of myself sitting on my couch with a toothbrush in hand, then I typed a caption:

2016 has been a tough year. In January I was hit by a car and broke my back. The recovery has been gruelling but after having broken my back once before this and losing the love of my life to suicide in 2012 I realised that kindness saved me then, and I'm hoping it can again. At 8 am on 12 August 2016 I am going to leave my home with nothing but the clothes on my back. No cash, credit card, food or water—I'm going to be reliant on the kindness of strangers to house me, feed me and get me from A to B. I won't accept help from family or friends. I'm convinced that the world is a really good place and I need you guys to help me prove that. Let's see how far I can go.

Pressing 'post' was actually really easy. I had thought I would be nervous putting myself out there so publicly, to be potentially rejected or criticised, but I wasn't. I sat there after posting waiting to see if anyone responded, and was amazed at the speed with which responses started coming in. Within minutes there were hundreds of likes and too many shares to remember. Best friends, teammates from way back—but also strangers who were inspired by what I was hoping to do.

I put myself to bed that night and fell asleep with relative ease—which was a surprise, because I hadn't been sleeping well. I woke up early the next day and immediately checked my phone. There were hundreds of texts and missed calls that had come through when I'd been asleep, and when I logged on to my social media pages, the notifications were going off. My post had gone viral, and thousands of people were reaching out to help me.

Remembering the smile that crept onto my face in that moment still brings me such joy. I hadn't even left yet, but the journey had already proven to me that kindness did still exist. The world is a pretty incredible place.

I spent the next few days hearing from various media outlets and friends and family. All of them said they were blown away by what I was doing. A Channel Seven news reporter, Robert Ovadia, wanted to do a story to help me get the word out there, and so a few days later I found myself filming a segment that would be shown on primetime news bulletins and during the broadcast of the 2016 Olympic Games in Rio!

After the segment aired, I was contacted by thousands of people from all around the world. I received offers of cash, of transport to wherever I needed to go, and of all sorts of accommodation. I had so many offers that I had to ask some friends to come around and help me filter through them all, to try to map out a plan.

My phone would not stop ringing, and my friends wrote out the offers on sheets of paper, laying them out on the polished floorboards of my apartment. I remember being amazed at the sheer volume of scattered pieces of paper—at one point I had to stand on the lounge to be able to see them all clearly.

We categorised the offers in geographical groups. Offers from New South Wales were towards the door, Victorians who had reached out were over near my kitchen, Queenslanders were in the middle of my lounge room and the rest were in my spare bedroom. There were little pieces of paper with notes like:

> Mick, Brunswick, Vic.—Can put you up with his family (spare bed)—whatever food you need.
> Sue, Cronulla, NSW—Can drive you around Sydney on the 16th Aug if needed.
> Amanda, Fremantle, WA—Invited you to the Bunnings to help cook snags (and eat them) and happy to put you up.

It wouldn't be long before I was leaving, so I spent the next few days trying to organise myself in the safest way possible. There was a whirlwind of media, farewells from friends and family, and of course planning the trip ahead. I pulled together a rough itinerary of what my first week might look like, ensured that my pet turtles would be looked after, and said my final goodbyes to my closest family and friends.

Of the thousands of offers I received before leaving, many stood out to me. Not because they were grand or lavish, but because the people making them had shared a little about themselves and why they wanted to help me. I knew that these were the types of people I wanted to be spending my time with.

And it was hearing from people like this that made me suspect this journey was going to change my life.

The things I learned as I travelled have become the framework by which I now live my life. And whenever I need reminding that there is hope even in the darkest of places, I only have to reach for one of these memories, as they perfectly showcase the kindness of so-called strangers.

Before I had this experience, I knew that human connection was important, but it was while travelling that I came to see just how vital it really is. Not just for me, but for everyone.

• • •

As far back as I can remember, I've always had a keen interest in people and human behaviour. It's always struck me how similar we are—yet how unique each of us is at the same time. How our experiences and those with whom we are lucky enough to share our lives can shape us, and help us to see the world in a particular way. As a kid, I didn't really understand what that all meant, but I'm told I was thought of as a curious and empathetic child.

I had a pretty normal childhood. I am the youngest of four kids, and the only girl. Mum and Dad are from working-class families, and the work ethic that was instilled in them by their parents was definitely passed on to my brothers and me. If there's one thing you couldn't criticise a Koschel of, it's being lazy. We simply don't know how to sit still.

Mum and Dad met in Sydney, but both are from remote areas of New South Wales. Budgets were tight when I was growing up, and our family holidays were almost always to Finley to visit Nanna and Pa. We didn't have any big international or even interstate trips, but I never once felt like I was missing out, even when my classmates in high school told me about visiting Disneyland or castles in London.

My favourite memories as a child are of Finley. It's a really sleepy town with a population of about 1500. Back then, it had a fish and chip shop, two pubs, an RSL and a swimming pool that cost about $1.20 for a day ticket. That's where my brothers and I would spend most of our time—unless the cricket was on. Then we would have it blaring on the TV at

Nanna and Pa's, and during the lunch and tea breaks we would go out in the backyard and pretend that we were the players on the screen.

My love of sport really developed in Finley, because there was less distraction from devices like computers and video games, and the best way to entertain yourself was to get outside and run around.

I'm not sure exactly when I fell in love with the game of cricket. Perhaps it was during my first competitive match, or maybe even before then, when I was playing with my older brothers and chasing the ball around the backyard. What I can safely say is that my love of the game has never been lost to me.

As far back as I can remember, all I ever wanted to be was a cricket player. My dreams and aspirations as a girl became reality as a young adult in 2011, when I made my debut for New South Wales. Playing for my state was one of the most euphoric feelings I can remember, especially as I'd had to work so hard to be there.

Pa, my dad's father, is probably one of my favourite people on the planet. He's the ultimate gentleman—I can only describe his love for Nanna as like something out of a Disney movie. They were madly in love with each other, and Pa wasn't afraid to share that with anyone who would listen. I can't remember a meal that we shared where he didn't pull her chair out for her and kiss her fondly on the cheek as she sat down. Whenever they walked together they held hands.

Seeing that always melted my heart, especially when I became an adult with more life experience. When I was a kid, I just saw it as Nanna and Pa being Nanna and Pa, but as I look back, I see everything they taught me simply by just being themselves. Now I understand how rare it is to have a front-row seat to a love story like theirs.

Pa and Nanna never pretended to be anyone other than themselves, and I like to think that they passed this form of self-acceptance down to me. What Pa taught me through his actions is that integrity is everything, and your word is your word. This would come in handy in my adult years, when I needed strong principles to guide my decisions.

I've always loved that I can say I have family in Finley. Part of me wishes it was my home. Every time I'm there, I almost instantly feel a sense of calmness, and time seems to stop. Finley has always felt like home, and I know now that that's because home is where your people are. The ones who love you the most.

It's not the town, or the pub or the high school that make Finley feel that way. It's Nanna and Pa, Mum and Dad in holiday mode and my brothers and me mucking around together. It's the people on the street who know you as Gary's daughter, or as Ray and Marie's granddaughter who plays cricket and swims in the pool almost every day. And I know that this sense of home and security can be found anywhere, even in the most unlikely places—and even with friends you've only just met.

I know this because I felt that same homely feeling on the very first day of my kindness journey. And on the second day, and the day after that. In fact, I felt it every day for two whole months.

Self-acceptance

It was 7.50 am on Friday, 12 August, and I was running late. I ushered Mum and Dad out of the house with me, and noticed a small teardrop on Mum's cheek. While I was aware that heading out on this journey could be the worst decision of my life to date, I also knew it might be the best thing I would ever do for myself.

But as I pulled the door shut behind me, all my nervous energy melted away. I knew that everything was going to be okay. In fact, I had never been surer of anything in my life. People are good.

The first leg of my journey was via train from Mortdale, in Sydney's south-west, into the city. I was met at the train station by more family and one of my best friends, Corinne, who offered me a can of deodorant to take with me as a way to lighten the mood. My nephews wished me well on my 'holiday' and promised to look after my turtles, Twix and Finley. It was an emotional time for everyone, but we were all excited too.

Up the stairs I went, doing a quick mental check of my backpack as I ascended:

- Toothbrush
- Spare pair of jeans and hoodie
- Empty water bottle
- Phone and charger

My bag was pretty light, but I knew it would fill up quickly as my journey progressed. I was about to leave my home with almost nothing. No cash, no cards, no food or water, and no help from immediate family or friends. I would be reliant on the kindness of strangers to survive. What on earth was I doing? And why did it feel so right?

I got to the top of the stairs and turned around to see Dad with his arm around Mum, trying to reassure her, I think. I went down another set of stairs to the platform and found a seat on the station while I waited for my train to arrive. As I started to think about who I was due to meet, I became distracted by Mum and my nephews, who were shouting to get my attention. We blew each other kisses and waved, and then they disappeared as the train pulled in.

This is me. Off I go.

I didn't even have a train ticket when I boarded—I had to trust that my first stranger, Tmne (pronounced 'Tem-knee'), would meet me at Bondi station and hand me a ticket so I could get through the turnstile.

Organisation has never been a strength of mine, so filtering through the 10,000 offers from people who had reached out to help me was a challenge. Thankfully, my army of supportive friends had helped me enormously, and I'd had some good advice from an adventurer that I took as gospel: 'Never go to bed without knowing where you will be sleeping the next night.'

With that in mind, my friends and I had pieced together a loose itinerary: who I would meet first, and how I would get myself safely to the Northern Beaches that night and have a warm bed to sleep in.

Although Tmne was a stranger to me, she had followed the journey of the Kindness Factory since it had started just under a year earlier, so it didn't take long after she gave me my ticket at Bondi station for her to seem very familiar. To kick off my journey in style, Tmne had organised breakfast for me, and invited a small group of women—some of her closest friends—to join us.

At a cosy Bondi cafe, I ordered smashed avocado on toast and an almond flat white. An array of warm drinks—some so fancy that I'd never heard of them—were delivered to our table for the others. The conversation immediately focused on me, and immediately I was out of my comfort zone as I filled them in on my life to date. Some had heard my story, while others hadn't. In minutes we were all on the verge of tears, but already we felt connected by something bigger.

I was amazed to learn more about each person, and discovered that I was in some incredible company. Magistrates, barristers, lawyers and charity workers—they all had important things to say, and I was fascinated by them. Tmne had to leave early as she was volunteering at the local breast cancer support centre, so two of the other ladies produced goodie bags with food, pyjamas and water they'd brought for me. I was grateful—and my bag was already much heavier than when I'd left home that morning.

The ladies chipped in and donated some cash to get me by for a while. It was hard for me to accept but they insisted, and I knew it would come in handy if I ran into any trouble.

Eventually I said goodbye to the crew and headed outside. It was raining so I walked into the nearby Westfield for some shelter. I had done a lot of work with homeless communities in the past three years, and my mind kept thinking about the people I'd met—it struck me now that there wasn't much difference between them and me. Not just because I was now literally homeless and reliant on strangers to survive, but also because almost every homeless person I had met had a story of extreme adversity.

But I knew, deep down, that our experiences weren't the same. What I was doing was a social experiment, and I could pull out of it at any moment. And I had support networks in place, people who would ensure that I never fell through the cracks.

I realised then that I should consider myself the luckiest person in the world. People had always shown up for me. Kindness had always been present, even when I faced adversity—at least, I had always seen it that way. And, after all, that was why I'd begun this journey in the first place. Kindness had saved my life once before—so why couldn't it do so again?

• • •

When I first envisioned this trip, I imagined lots of hitchhiking and walking to get from A to B, and that I'd be meeting all sorts of people along the way. The reality pulled up to the kerb after my breakfast with Tmne: a sleek luxury car driven by Paul, a curious and down-to-earth man who had offered to drive me around for however long I'd be in Sydney. On day one he took me from Bondi to Parramatta, and then into the CBD, and finally to Fairlight, in the Northern Beaches, and he waited for me as I met people and organisations in between.

As I sat in the leather passenger seat and Paul turned on the seat warmer, I could only shake my head in wonder. The ridiculousness of the situation was not lost on me. To go from feeling like I was at rock bottom to being chauffeured around Sydney thanks to the goodwill of others might seem absurdly privileged, and perhaps even selfish, but in committing to this journey I had made a deal with myself: I would accept help from people in whatever form it came to me. That was something I had always wrestled with in the past. The company Paul worked for had seen me on the news and reached out to offer transport while I was in Sydney. It was incredibly generous, and I'm not sure I would have got through my first couple of days on the road if not for this kindness. I sure as hell wouldn't have been as comfortable.

As far back as I can remember, I've had a fierce need for independence—and I am stubborn to a fault. These aren't things that I'm necessarily proud of, but I know these imperfections are a key part of me. Each of us has strengths and areas that we need to work on.

My stubbornness and need for independence come, I think, from my childhood. Being the youngest kid in the family and the only girl, I always felt I had something to prove to my brothers. I had to be strong—physically but also emotionally—so I could take part in their antics. If I fell over and scraped my knee, I wouldn't dare let them see me upset.

29

It would have meant I couldn't join in whatever game we were playing—they would have deemed it something only boys could do. I took pride in my attitude from a young age, and it remained with me as an adult. I pretty much mastered the art of stubbornness—I'd been practising my entire life.

There is nothing inherently wrong with being stubborn, of course, but when a quality like that is so ingrained, it can become a problem: you can struggle to control the power it has over you. I've found, however, that when I'm aware of my imperfections, I have been able to use them as superpowers. That is why self-awareness is something I've consciously sought, mostly by assessing my own actions but also via trusted friends who have offered feedback and advice.

So self-awareness, in my experience, is often the first step to finding and maintaining self-acceptance. I say 'maintaining' because we, as human beings, are always changing and growing, and self-acceptance needs to be practised almost daily for it to contribute to your life and happiness.

Cricket wasn't always easy for me. The number of knock-backs I had in my very short career would have convinced most people to walk away and focus on a career that would help pay the bills. But not me—I loved it too much.

Someone who spotted that love was a very dear friend of mine, Beth Morgan, who played international cricket for England. It was Beth who gave me my first opportunity as a professional in the United Kingdom, and I spent the 2008 and 2009 seasons at Middlesex as their overseas player. It was the first time I had really lived away from home, and I grew up a lot in those two years. When I came back to Sydney, I had a stronger case to present to the selectors in New South Wales.

My first season back on Australian soil playing for my beloved St George-Sutherland was a standout, and I was selected to play for New South Wales in January 2011. When I got the news, I can't remember who I told first. I think it was Nanna and Pa back in Finley, and then probably Mum and Dad and my brothers.

I'd had a great Second XI carnival in Canberra in the December before this selection, scoring the most runs in the competition. What none of us realised during that period was that I was actually battling a pretty serious injury in my spine. I had noticed symptoms prior to the selection and went to consult with our team physio, Kate.

The physio's room was fairly unfamiliar to me, because I'd never liked making a fuss about injuries. The summer before, I had played an entire tour of New Zealand with a broken thumb. I'd hurt it a couple of weeks before leaving, but didn't want to miss out, so I told no one. I played terribly, though, and when I eventually had scans, they revealed a break that was so bad I had to have surgery.

I still experience problems with that thumb to this day, and I know it will only get worse with age. This is one example of my stubbornness being detrimental to my health and happiness.

Anyway, when I went to see Kate, she was a little shocked to see me and asked what was going on. I explained that I had a sharp pain in my left leg, from my buttock down through to my calf. I also mentioned that my left big toe was numb—I hadn't been able to feel it for the best part of a month.

She asked me to hop onto the bed and assessed me. Her silence was a little worrying, but those worries were soon alleviated by the humour that my teammates took from the lack of feeling in my big toe.

'What do you mean you can't feel it?' they asked.

'I just can't,' I said, as if it were the most normal thing in the world.

Kate examined me for about 30 minutes, then asked me to head down to the gym. She ordered a scan through our team doctor the next day, and told me I was on light duties for the time being. No running, no drills—I was only allowed to sit on the stationary bike. I got into a bit of strife when she came down about an hour later and saw me in the nets bowling to a few of my teammates. I left training that night with a referral letter, disappointed that I wasn't able to train the way that I wanted to.

The scans I had the next day revealed that I had a prolapsed disc in my spine. What that meant was that part of my disc had started to slip out of the surrounding vertebrae and was pressing on some of the nearby nerves. The prolapse was significant enough to cause concern, I was told, but not so bad as to be dangerous. It was up to me to decide whether I was fit for my debut match for New South Wales in a week's time.

I was well informed of the potential risks of playing with my injury. My doctor was even kind enough to introduce me to the former Test fast bowler Brett Lee to ponder the decision with. Brett happened to be the appointment after mine in the medical room of the SCG that day and when he arrived early for a prearranged injection, my doctor thought it might be handy for me to have a chat. We introduced ourselves and began mentally jotting down the pros and cons of playing. Brett was cautious. 'You only get one spine, Kath.' But even with his advice, the decision was easy for me. I had been offered the chance to live out my childhood dream and represent my state in the sport that I loved the most. I'd been dreaming of this moment since I was an eight-year-old girl. I let the selectors know I was in.

Two days later, the teams were announced, with me as an opening batter for New South Wales. We were due to travel to the Adelaide Oval for a series of matches against South Australia. To say I was excited would be an understatement.

I didn't sleep much in the leadup to our departure. Partly because I was so excited, but also because the pain in my leg was now so bad that sleep was almost impossible. The numbness in my toe had also got worse. I couldn't feel most of my left foot by this time, and I had started to notice symptoms that I later learned were the early stages of a condition called foot drop.

Foot drop means that dorsiflexion—the ability to lift your toes—is almost impossible, or at least very limited. For me this meant playing cricket shots had become more and more difficult, and running between the wickets was painful.

We defeated South Australia in the first game—and, despite my physical limitations, the 57 I scored in a player-of-the-match performance meant it was a fairytale debut.

At the time, I thought it was the greatest day of my life. I felt euphoric. To have worked so hard for something and then to play like that is an almost unbeatable feeling as an athlete. And in hindsight, I'm so glad that I experienced that moment, because my cricket career was about to be over only moments after it started. I lasted just four games before my condition deteriorated further, to the point that surgery was my only option.

I had four attempts at less dramatic and invasive surgeries before I learned of a new surgery called a total disc replacement. In 2011, the surgery was only being attempted by one surgeon in Australia, who worked on the Gold Coast, in Queensland.

A few days after hearing about some of the results he had seen in athletes, I was in his office completing an assessment.

After a long consultation and many questions, we agreed that I was a suitable candidate for the operation. It was a tough moment for me when I had to acknowledge that this was probably the only chance that I would have of ever walking again.

A date for the operation was set not long after that, and I had a conversation with my parents to see if one of them could make the trip with me to the Gold Coast. The surgery was just the first hurdle I needed to get over—the early stages of rehabilitation and physiotherapy on the Gold Coast were some of the several other hurdles that I would need to clear, and I knew there was no way I could do it alone.

Dad agreed to take the next six weeks off work. He would fly with me and then support me in hospital and once I was set up in our accommodation, which would be our home until I was medically cleared to fly back to Sydney.

Two weeks after that initial consultation, I was in Labrador, on the Gold Coast, preparing for the surgery the next day. It had been an intense build-up, and nervousness and doubt had started to set in. I'd done my pre-scans, had a consultation with the physio I would be working with for the next six weeks, and all the necessary measurements had been taken.

I remember feeling quite excited when I learned that I would grow approximately four centimetres taller as a result of the procedure. It was height that I had lost because of my injury, but nonetheless this fact blew my mind. *How amazing is the human body,* I kept thinking.

So I was as physically prepared for that surgery as I could ever be—but I hadn't considered my emotional and mental health.

My memories of waking from the surgery are a blur of extreme physical pain, a lot of medications that affected my thinking, and genuine fear that I had made a very big error in having the operation. A common question after a surgery is your pain score, which is rated from one to ten. It takes a lot for me to acknowledge that anything is bothering me above a five. After coming out of the surgery, I even surprised myself when I answered, through gritted teeth, that my pain score was at seven out of ten.

I felt like I spent the hours and days following the surgery going between consciousness and unconsciousness. My heart rate was naturally low due to my fitness as a professional athlete, and that, coupled with the unfamiliar drugs going through my system, meant that I felt a lot of noise and clutter in my mind, which I later discovered was a mild form of situational anxiety.

Despite having been told I might never walk again—because even with the surgery, nothing was guaranteed—up until this point I honestly still thought I would be back out on the park playing cricket again in the not-too-distant future.

This was where my awareness of my own strengths and weaknesses came in handy. When used in a healthy way, there is nothing wrong with being stubborn, but it was important for me to know when to tap into my stubbornness and when to bypass it. Self-awareness and self-acceptance, I have learned, are crucial for facing what life throws at us.

As the days went on, my new-found anxieties began to swell. Not only did my dream of playing cricket again feel like it was slipping further and further away, I was becoming more unsure if I would ever walk again. This prospect was staring me in the face almost every day.

After what felt like weeks, but in reality was only a few days, I was able to incline my bed enough that I could see my room—I'd been staring at the roof as I laid there in traction following the surgery. I was as stiff as a board, but I was also determined. Several practitioners at the hospital guided my feet to the floor and I managed to stand for the first time and take my first steps.

I only took two steps that day, and I still had no feeling in either of my legs, but the day after that I took four steps, and the day after that I took eight.

The next four weeks flew by as the fear of the unknown of my situational anxiety lifted and things became much clearer in my thought process. At the six-week mark of recovery, I had my final check-up and was given the all-clear to fly back to Sydney and continue my rehab at home. By this point I was walking with the help of a set of forearm crutches, and no one could have guessed how severe the prognosis I'd faced was.

Back in Sydney, I returned to work a few days per week—a part-time role coaching kids and setting up cricket matches—and was continuing my recovery with the help of specialists and physios who kept me on track. At the twelve-week mark of my recovery, I had to fly back to the Gold Coast for a follow-up consultation. My surgeon was thrilled with my progress, which saw me walking without any assistance, albeit a little slow and gingerly.

In the car heading for Coolangatta airport, where I was to board my flight back to Sydney, my mind began entertaining the idea of cricket again and what that might look like. I set my sights on playing for New South Wales again. It was a bold target, but one that I didn't think was out of reach.

It is in moments like these that I really appreciate my stubbornness. Looking back now, I know that it was an ambitious goal, but at the time I backed myself. I knew I had the work ethic to get me to where I wanted to go, and I was willing to fight for it.

A few days later I woke up at 4 am with no feeling in my left leg. This was an unusual setback, but as I lay there trying to move my toes, I assured myself that I must have slept on it strangely. After waiting a little while with no improvement, I took matters into my own hands. I picked up my lifeless left leg with my hands and swung it off the bed. Surely I just needed to get some blood flow back into it, I thought. I stood up as best as I could—and the next thing I knew I was on the floor. I'd collapsed under the weight of my body, my left leg unable to take the load.

I was due in rehab early that morning for a routine appointment, but my appointment was still at least two hours away. I managed to get myself dressed, then crawled past my flatmates' bedrooms and into my car. My right leg was working alright, so I started driving towards what I thought would be rehab. It seemed like the best option at the time. It was a 24-hour facility and so amidst the panic I was feeling, I figured if I got there early, surely someone who knew of my injuries would be able to help me. On the way there, I called my doctor and explained my situation to him. He said straightaway that I should bypass rehab and meet him at the Royal Prince Alfred Hospital.

I parked my car in the emergency bay and, not wanting to alarm anyone, crawled into the emergency department. The triage nurse looked very confused to see me dragging myself through the emergency doors on my elbows, but she immediately sprang into action and helped me into a wheelchair.

I began explaining what I had experienced over the past six months, and how I had woken up that day without feeling in my leg. More and more doctors came into the consultation room—I remember feeling rather like a farm animal, as the doctors poked and prodded and ordered tests.

Eventually, one doctor came in to confirm what seemed to be on everyone's mind. I could tell the news wasn't going to be good: the expressions on all the faces were grave, and no one could maintain eye contact with me. Even so, I never anticipated what the doctor was about to say.

'Kath, we're afraid the news is not great. We are going to amputate your leg.'

'Pardon?' I replied, almost sarcastically—I simply could not believe what they were telling me.

'We've done all the tests that we can possibly think to do, and the best course of action right now is for you to have your leg amputated.'

How had I gone from contemplating once again playing professional sport only days earlier to being told I would lose my entire left leg? I simply wasn't prepared to hear this—no one had ever told me this was a risk.

I pleaded for an explanation but was left disappointed, so I decided to call my brother Grant to ask for help. Grant and I have always been close and he is also one of the most positive people I know. I think I needed to let someone in to share the load with—and to hear what I knew would be positive words.

He was shocked when I told him what was happening— but not as much as I was, having been in the thick of it all morning. How could this be happening? It made absolutely no sense to me or Grant—nor to the doctors, it seemed. I remember pleading with them, only to be stared at blankly as if they were trying to come up with a solution on the spot.

Finally, after much discussion, the doctors agreed to give me two weeks to try to recover without amputation. Because there was a blood-flow issue, they would have to monitor me closely, and if my blood pressure dropped too low, my leg would have to be amputated. Keeping it moving would give me the best possible chance.

In 2011, being a female athlete wasn't really celebrated in mainstream society. We worked hard every day at training and in our lives—we gave up financial security, a social life and sometimes even study to do what we did. Some of us even had to pay for the privilege of competing for our state.

Now, I saw, that dedication would give me the best chance at keeping my leg. I would need to perform. My leg depended on it. Win or lose, I would give it my all. I was already proud of myself for that decision.

• • •

As Paul and I planned our meeting spots for the rest of our day, he asked me about Lucy, who I was meeting for dinner in Darling Harbour. 'What's her story?' he asked with curiosity. Paul had already become somewhat protective of me, and I knew he was asking for the right reasons.

Sitting with Lucy that evening in one of the fanciest restaurants I had ever been to was a real treat. As we looked out over the glistening water in front of us and tucked in to some of the best Thai food imaginable, I had to pinch myself.

Lucy wasn't a complete stranger. We had met once before—she'd been the recipient of the first ever act of kindness I did in what went on to become the Kindness Factory. She'd seen my story on the news recently and reached out.

As we chatted, Lucy noticed that a famous footballer had walked right by our table. She was giving me the eye and nodding her head towards him, but I was missing her cue entirely. As the footballer left the restaurant, she proclaimed, 'Did you not just see Buddy Franklin?'

'No, I didn't,' I said.

'I was kicking you the entire time he was standing there!'

'Oh, I can't feel my leg,' I replied. Lucy looked utterly confused. 'It's one of the residual effects from my injuries. I didn't know you were kicking me!'

Lucy almost looked saddened by this, but I reassured her that I was fine with it—I had learned quite quickly to live with it and accept it for what it was.

'But how do you walk?' Lucy asked.

'With a lot of practice, failure and falls.'

It was interesting to me how fascinated Lucy was by the difference she had just learned about in me. So often when we meet people, we look for connection. The way we look, or how we speak and behave. When I was in primary school, I remember seeing someone very close to me get bullied for their lack of interest in sport—they preferred to study frogs and other insects, harming no one or nothing in the process. I often asked myself: why were they bullied? This child was much more than their lack of interest in sport—they had a beautiful personality.

Similarly, I think I was able to show Lucy, through my acceptance of my more limited abilities, that I too was more than my numb leg—I didn't see my disability as a hindrance, as able-bodied people might. Learning to live with my disability wasn't all doom and gloom. Because of it, I have met many wonderful people who have also learned to live with their difference, and my life has only become richer in the process.

• • •

My next two weeks were a whirlwind, with a lot of up-and-down emotions.

A routine day consisted of getting up at about 4 am and eating breakfast, then heading to the hospital or rehab centre

43

to have everything tested to ensure my health and leg were stable. After that I'd head to work for a few hours, then I'd go home and eat something, then head to my local gym and train with a personal trainer I had enlisted to help. I'd go back home, eat more food and then head back to the gym and get my leg moving in any way that I could.

My situation was confronting not only for me but for anyone who saw me trying to get by. I was back on crutches, and as I would hop around on my healthy right leg, my left leg would drag behind me, apparently lifeless. After eating dinner I was always anxious about how well I would sleep.

Since I had been on the New South Wales cricket team, I had 24-hour access to the Sydney Cricket Ground. One night, after tossing and turning in bed for a few hours, I drove to Moore Park and set myself up as best I could in the fitness centre. I turned the lights on at two in the morning, thinking I was the only person who would notice, but I was soon met by a curious security guard, Bobby, who knew there shouldn't be anyone in the gym at that hour, let alone someone trying to train.

I explained my situation to Bobby, though I was sure he would kick me out. There were no rules about when you could and couldn't visit that facility, which was owned by Cricket NSW, but I was pretty certain they didn't want anyone there at 2 am.

Bobby met me with kindness and empathy. He saw my need for help, and rather than kicking me out, which he would definitely have been entitled to do, he helped me.

Bobby wasn't a doctor or a specialist. But in that moment, I didn't need either of those. In that moment I needed someone to show up for me, and I needed someone to care—and that's what he did.

Bobby went back to his post and came back a few moments later with some electrical tape. I was confused at first, but then he helped me onto a spin bike and literally taped my left leg to the pedal so I could keep it moving without anyone helping me. The gentleness of Bobby's actions made me feel safe, and I started to trust what he was suggesting. He headed back to his post for 45 minutes, then came back and untaped my foot and helped me down.

Bobby's actions taught me that it's okay to accept help. I realised that I couldn't fight this battle alone, and that sometimes my stubbornness and independence weren't actually helping me. It was the first time I acknowledged that if I was going to win this fight, I couldn't do it alone. This represented a real shift from a week earlier, when I'd crawled and dragged myself into hospital.

If I wanted to keep my leg attached, I now knew, I couldn't keep battling on alone. I had to ask myself: is my stubborn nature helping or hindering? In this instance, it was hindering, which meant that I had to adapt and learn to not go it alone.

I have to admit, this was a foreign concept and it felt awkward and unfamiliar—but most things do when we try them for the first time. And I've noticed that, especially when we're going against everything we know, we tend to grow the most because we are completely outside our comfort zone.

The gratitude I have for Bobby is immense, and his kindness to me in those moments is something I will never forget. There I was, in the fight of my life, and a stranger who saw my struggle had helped. It meant everything to me. If it ever crossed my mind to give up during that two-week period, I only had to think of Bobby and I would keep going.

My two weeks were due to finish on a Monday. The Friday before, I went in for my orthopaedic appointment and was confronted with the news that my efforts hadn't paid off, and that the best course of action was still to amputate. I think I knew that news was coming, so I felt somewhat prepared—and even, if you can believe it, a little bit relieved. The two weeks of fighting to keep my leg had completely worn me down, and I was exhausted. I knew I had given it a good fight. Walking out of that appointment, I had my head held high. I was determined to spend my last weekend with two legs not feeling sorry for myself.

There weren't too many people in my life, outside my immediate family and friends, who were aware of the prospect

I was facing. I hadn't chosen to keep things quiet—I'd simply gone from one traumatic thing to the next over a very short period of time, and I couldn't find the energy to inform more than my tight circle of the battle I was still fighting.

Knowing that I was due for surgery and no longer had to fight, I felt a weight shift off my shoulders that weekend. Finally I relaxed a little. I don't remember too much about what happened next, but I started to feel progressively more and more ill—to the point that I collapsed.

I was rushed to the nearest hospital, where further testing showed that I had been bleeding internally from one of the many surgeries I'd undergone. Due to my spinal cord injury, I had a very damaged nerve system in my left leg, and the limited supply of blood in my body simply wasn't getting into my left leg. Once the bleed was found, I was raced off for more surgery.

I woke up a few hours later and, in a drug-induced haze, began feeling around for my left leg. My stirring must have alerted the doctors, who began to come in to support me and explain what was going on. My leg was still attached, but I still couldn't feel it and from the way that it seemed to weigh my hip down, I knew it was still very lifeless and heavy. The bleed had been fixed and so there was hope of keeping my leg, but the damage to my leg and body was extensive. I was facing a week in hospital to start with and then the advice was that I should head to a rehabilitation centre for the indefinite future. To keep my leg healthy I still needed medical supervision, and I also needed help to start to relearn basic tasks like walking and self-care. When your leg is in that bad a shape, you'd be amazed at how big an impact it has on your life. Learning to walk was the most obvious of tasks ahead of me, but I hadn't considered things like how to balance with no feeling in one leg, showering, and how to care for a limb that now worked differently. Going home and caring for myself independently or without medical assistance simply wasn't an option. Not only was I still at risk of having my leg amputated if things went the wrong way, considering the extensive nerve damage I had that no one could unequivocally tell me would improve, but if I ever wanted to walk again then this was my only chance.

My stubbornness had saved my leg by propelling me through the last two weeks of gruelling effort. But stubbornness is not always the answer—sometimes we can't just muscle our way through a problem.

Self-acceptance is a work in progress.

Perspective

On day two of my journey, I was excited to get moving again. I'd stayed with a family called the Parks the night before, and had agreed to meet Claudia Vera at Circular Quay at 2 pm. By then she would have finished a march through the city streets in support of same-sex marriage.

I'd felt a whirlwind of emotions after my first day on the road: curiosity, excitement and even a few tears. If this was how the journey was going to play out, I thought, I was in for the experience of my life. In the morning, the Parks had made me feel like family, offering me a plethora of breakfast options, and I'd watched their children playing their Saturday sport.

As I waited for Claudia, I suddenly realised I didn't have her number stored in my phone. As I searched through the thousands of social media messages in my inboxes, I remembered why I was so excited to meet Claudia in the first place. Three members of her incredible family had reached out separately to offer help. When I was planning the first few days of my journey, I understood that these were people I needed to meet, to give me a dose of perspective.

It's hard to not feel emotional when I think about the incredible souls who make up the Vera family. When I was filtering through the thousands of offers to help me, I'd noted that they had shared part of their background as refugees, and I knew then that they had a story worth knowing.

Claudia appeared at 1.55 pm armed with a hug, a coffee and a heart full of love that I didn't know I needed at the time. I wanted to know more about this special woman. Claudia is impressive—she was a mother to a fifteen-month-old daughter at the time, and a wife to Danilo, and they were originally from Chile. Claudia worked for the NSW Teacher's Federation in Sydney and was passionate about standing up for people and justice.

Claudia took me straight to her father's workplace—a second-hand office furniture factory—where I was greeted by Sergio. I was confused at first about why we went there, rather than to her family home, where I would be staying that night. I asked Claudia, but she simply replied that her father had requested this. He wanted to show me his workplace, and from the tour he gave me, I could tell he was tremendously proud of what he did.

And so he should have been. Serg was very well known in the community, and people wouldn't just visit him for furniture but for good conversation. We hugged for what felt like ten minutes. He was so friendly and caring, welcoming me into his factory and showing me all sorts of things—chairs, tables, doors, antiques. You name it, it was there.

As we got chatting, I learned more about this special man's life, and Sergio explained to me why he was so happy to be in this country with his beautiful family. It almost broke me to hear what this man and his family had been through.

In 1984, Sergio had been wrongfully imprisoned and tortured for over thirteen months by the Chilean dictatorship. His sentence of 'four years and one day' had a particular meaning: after four years in jail, it was guaranteed that he would go missing on that 'one day'. He told me how, in support, the Archbishop of the Catholic Church assigned him a lawyer from the Vicariate of Solidarity to fight for his release. He sought asylum through Amnesty International, and his wife Iris was faced with the life-altering decision about whether to leave the country with him. She left it all; they left together. I hadn't met Iris yet but I knew just by how Serg and Claud had been speaking about her that she was someone special.

What struck me most about this family was their caring and gentle nature. I remember thinking that they seemed like the happiest and most grounded people I'd ever met, even though that didn't match what I was learning about their past. I felt so welcomed by them all, and the longer Sergio and I kept chatting, the safer I began to feel, as if I had known them for years. They felt like family.

My moments of feeling lost, vulnerable and afraid in the leadup to this journey had vanished as I enjoyed the feeling of being home again—a home away from home.

I jumped back in the car with Claud and she told me what it was like growing up. When her parents had to leave Chile and come to Australia, Claudia was just two years old. The family left with one bag containing three blankets and little else.

Hearing this made the journey I was on seem trivial, but Claudia never made me feel that way. Learning of their struggle gave me more perspective, but also more and more admiration and respect for the people her family had chosen to be, despite the hardship that they'd been through to get here.

Claud had learned two languages—one at school and one at home. She told me how she wrote notes to the teachers on behalf of her parents as they weren't able to at first. While she was talking, her daughter Victoria, sitting in the back seat, started to cry. Claud began singing and immediately Victoria was calm. She was a wonderful mother who adored her daughter, and it was easy to see how much love infused the entire family.

We got to Claud and Danilo's home in Camden, in Sydney's south-west, and I was introduced to Iris, Sergio's wife. She was beautiful and caring, a Spanish teacher at a local public school in Ambarvale, where she'd worked for over 25 years. We connected immediately.

Danilo, Claud's husband, arrived home after his day at work and greeted me with a hug. We headed out to the deck, where the conversation turned to me. I shared with them how I'd come to this point in my life, what had led me to start the Kindness Factory and why I was on the journey. We cried together, for all that had been lost and for what life would hold for us down the track.

At one point Iris whispered to me how she 'loves so many things'. This life is all about love, I reflected. To love and to be loved. That's what it all comes down to. I knew I would take a lot from this amazing family. The simple approach to life they have is something I will hold on to forever.

Next the food began to appear—and there was plenty of it. *Pichanga*, a Chilean starter, *choricillos, asado, pebre* and *ensalada Chilena,* followed by *tres leches,* cakes that were decorated with words of kindness. That seemed appropriate, not because of my journey, but because this family were so kind. The food was like nothing I'd ever eaten before.

We chatted some more, and I felt incredibly lucky to be there. It was a Saturday night in Sydney and I was in amazing company—how could I feel anything but incredibly grateful for where this journey had already taken me?

Eventually family members began preparing for bed, and Serg and I were the only two left at the table. Now our conversation started to get a little deeper. The more we chatted, the more I began to understand about this man and his family's story. We were very different people in our backgrounds, but we agreed there and then that we were also very similar— we were both human beings who had been through their fair share of adversity.

Serg was curious about my life and why I was doing what I was. I had given him my usual spiel already, but he wanted to know more. I trusted him and felt safe, so I decided to dig a bit deeper. The only thing that had been holding me back was a fear of getting emotional and upset.

Serg interrupted my thoughts by asking simply how I was going. Immediately I found myself struggling to answer. Until this point in my journey, I had felt completely fine. And I was fine now as well. But no one had asked me this question in a long time, mostly because everyone was so caught up in the adventure of what I was doing. There was also something about the way Serg spoke that made me soften enough to answer his question truthfully.

I shook my head. But I think Serg already knew that I probably had a few things on my mind.

As we looked each other in the eye, I asked him, 'How do you do it, Serg? How do you stay so strong after everything you've been through?'

'We have to choose to wake up happy,' he said.

He spoke with such poise, and I reflected on how overcomplicated we tend to make things. It was a shift in perspective that I needed to hear. To get out of my own head and my own way of finding happiness. Yes, I had been through a lot, but ultimately it was my choice to wake up and make each day count. I alone was accountable for my own actions and happiness.

I now consider happiness to be a conscious choice every single day. I later learned that Serg reinforces this choice by his actions. He has a bad back and lives in chronic pain, so getting out of bed most days is a battle. The first thing he does every morning, though, is stand in front of the mirror and say, 'God, I'm handsome!' It makes his family laugh and sets a positive tone for the day.

As I went to bed that night with a grateful heart, I couldn't help but think of someone very close to me—a woman I'd met on my very first night in rehab. Her story, although very different from that of Sergio, Iris, Claudia and their family, also taught me a valuable lesson about perspective—and about how kindness, like happiness, is a choice.

• • •

On my first night in rehab in 2011, I woke to a dull drone of wailing from someone nearby. I immediately thought it must be an elderly woman, because I was temporarily in the geriatric ward—there were no free beds yet in the west wing, which would become my rehab home.

I pressed the call button near my bed. I don't normally like making a fuss, but this seemed important. When the nurse came in, I asked her if everything was okay. She just told me to rest up—I had a big day ahead tomorrow—and closed the door to my room.

But now I was hearing a commotion outside, as the noise from the old woman became louder. I felt for her. The wailing wasn't the type you might hear from someone who was complaining—there was a sadness about it, and she sounded as if she was deeply hurting.

I waited an hour or so, trying to sleep but unable to. I could still sense the woman's sadness, but her wailing was softer than before. I shifted myself into an upright position, which was quite a task, given the state that my body was in, and shifted myself into the wheelchair positioned by the right side of my bed. I didn't want to alert anyone to what I was about to do, and I remember feeling shocked at the elegance with which I placed myself into that chair—with hardly any sound at all.

It was about 3 am, and I was wide awake. I crept slowly in my chair towards the door, unlatched the handle, then wheeled myself into the corridor. I only had to go a few metres until I reached the woman whose cries had been consuming me for the past hour.

She saw me almost instantly, and her head shrank down into her pillow. Her tears were soft, but they continued flowing as she stared at me. As if on autopilot, I wheeled slowly into her room until I was right next to her. We didn't speak. I can't recall if I was worried someone might have heard us, but I now prefer to think that the moment was actually perfect without words. Because it was.

As I sat there next to her, I realised that this room was the place I needed to be right now. My fears and worries— about being in this environment and the injuries I had to recover from—had felt so daunting, but they immediately evaporated. When I reached out to hold her hand, I suddenly knew that everything would be okay. I would get through this, just as I had the many other challenges I'd faced in my life.

I learned the next day that the woman had dementia and had also recently suffered a stroke. I wondered for months why she called me Alice. I thought it was a nickname she'd spontaneously given me, and so in return I gave her the nickname Daisy. But I later learned that I had reminded her of her granddaughter,

Alice, who was a similar age to me. I cried when I realised that she thought I actually was her granddaughter.

Daisy, I noticed, didn't have too many visitors, but I like to think that I helped make up for that as we became the best of friends over the next twelve months. Little did I know that I was about to learn a great deal about myself, about the power of perspective and about human connection in the process.

It would be an understatement to say that my first week of rehab was tough, but thanks to Daisy, I never had to look too far for friendship. I quickly found a routine of physical rehab, but I also made sure to find time to see Daisy every day. At 3 pm we both had some down time in our schedule, so that became our hour together every day. I would take her a cup of tea—English breakfast with a dash of milk. She was fussy about her tea: a couple of drops too much milk and she would look at you in disgust. But I knew how much she looked forward to her cuppa every day.

Daisy had some awesome stories and always had me in fits of laughter. I was surprised how fast time passed when I was in her company. Her physical and mental disabilities often made her hard to understand, but if you listened closely, you would be rewarded. Three pm became the time I looked forward to most every day.

As great as friends like Daisy were, it wasn't long before the reality of my situation hit me, and I found myself questioning how on earth I was going to recover well enough to walk again. In physical therapy sessions, I was always frustrated by how slow the progress felt. I found myself with tears streaming down my face. *This is impossible*, I would think to myself.

In those moments, I had lost sight of what I was actually doing. What I needed was a friend to help me see clearly again—to give me a new perspective.

One day I called Erin in tears, asking her to come and pick me up. She was confused, as she knew I had a lengthy stay ahead of me.

'Ez, I don't think I can stay here much longer,' I said through sobs.

My words even shocked me as they came out of my mouth. I was struggling to keep myself together enough to continue the conversation, but soon I gave up and began wailing. All I could hear from Erin was heavy breathing, and I knew that she was struggling to hear me this way.

'Kath, you've held it together for so long,' she said eventually. 'It's completely normal to feel this way.' By now she was upset too. 'It's breaking me to hear you like this. I just wish so much that I could take everything that you're going through away. If I could trade places with you, I would.'

This was such a big statement. I would never want that for Erin, but even her suggestion of it made me feel I wasn't alone. It made me realise that I was actually the lucky one—I had to find my way through the unknowns of learning to walk again, but maybe that was better than watching me do it and feeling powerless to help. Understanding Erin's perspective gave me the clarity I needed to get myself back on track.

With Erin's words ringing in my ears, I committed myself right there and then to my recovery and the process of learning to walk again. My mindset changed: there was only one person responsible for my future, I decided, and that person was me, so I had to put in the work.

Without Erin's perspective, I would have found it tremendously hard to have kindness and compassion for myself, and for others on the ward, including Daisy. So often we get caught up in our own head, and overwhelmed by the seemingly impossible struggle that we have in front of us. Finding a new perspective can be a gift—for ourselves and for others.

Learning to walk again when your prognosis is as bad as what mine was is no mean feat. But when you break a goal down into bite-sized pieces, anything becomes possible. First I outlined the process in my head, and then I wrote it down, and I kept those notes in my physical therapy bag to serve as a reminder. I would go from my bed to a wheelchair, from the chair to a walking frame, from the frame to crutches, from two crutches to a single crutch, then I'd take my first step and be on my way. Simple.

Not so much.

The recovery was absolutely gruelling, and I had to grit my teeth through most of it. But by around the four-week mark I started to find a groove. I put that down to a lot of things. The belief Erin instilled in me was one key factor, but I also looked around me. When I saw someone who was in better shape than me, I would think: *If they can, I can.* And I never had to search too hard to find someone who was far worse off than me. My heart would always go out to these people, and I'm sure the empathy I felt for them also gave me important perspective. *If I can, they can.*

When I was a little girl, my grandfather often said to me: 'You were born with two ears and one mouth. Listen more than you speak.' So often in life we get caught up in our own agendas and to-do lists that we forget to consider what's going on for the people around us. I am guilty of this myself. Regardless of the situation we're in, it's important to take a breath and listen to those around us. None of us has all the answers. Sometimes those closest to us can give us valuable perspective—if only we stop and listen.

• • •

I woke the next day to the cuddles of a very excited Victoria Larrain, whose room I was sleeping in. It was a nice way to start the first Sunday morning of my trip. Soon I noticed an unfamiliar voice in the kitchen: it was Claudia's sister, Denisse. When I went out to meet her, what struck me first was her beautiful smile and calm energy. We introduced ourselves with a warm hug and sat down for breakfast. Denisse is a talented fashion designer, and the clothes and dresses she creates are stunning.

The more time I spent with the Veras over that weekend, the more I learned about the power of perspective. As we walked through a local park, chatting and sipping on coffee, I wondered how I would leave this incredible family to go on to wherever my journey would take me next. But as tough as it was to leave them, I knew I would visit again and spend many more beautiful moments with them.

The Vera family remain close friends of mine to this day, although I don't see them nearly as much as I would like to. Sadly, only two years after we met, the wonderful Iris found out that she had an incurable brain tumour. In her dying days, I was fortunate to be invited again into the family home to spend some quality time with her and her family. I felt so privileged to be in her presence in those very precious moments. Even in their grief, they remained so beautifully warm. They danced, sang songs, told stories and loved each other. Most importantly, they cherished every moment they had together. And still, with the memory and legacy of Iris driving them, they remain as united and loving-of-life as ever.

PERSPECTIVE

At Iris's funeral, I noticed something that truly shows the man Sergio is. As we embraced tightly outside the church, I felt him sob into my chest, and it almost bowled me over. This man had just lost his wife, his 'compañera de vida', and I could feel his pain. I wanted him to know that I would be there for him, for as long as he needed.

After his moment of deep sadness, Sergio looked up. 'She would want us to be happy,' he said. 'We have that choice— let's go and eat.'

Even in his bleakest moment, Sergio chose to be grateful for what he had. That attitude didn't take away his sadness, but made it just a little more bearable.

I believe we all have that choice. That is the privilege of life.

Humility

I stood on the stage of a school hall in Goulburn with 500 kids staring up at me. I was nervous; I kept fidgeting with the pages of notes that I had quickly scribbled down the night before. I had never shared so much about my life in public before, let alone in front of hundreds of teenagers. My mouth felt dry and my hands were clammy.

I took a breath and thought back to the night before, when I'd said goodbye to the Veras, and the memory gave me strength. As soon as I opened my mouth to speak, my nerves began to dissipate. I could see Sal, the teacher who'd organised my visit, nodding encouragingly from the front row; the kids beside her looked curious and engaged. As I began telling them my story, I recognised that the room was hanging on to my every word.

As I neared the end of the talk, I could see a bunch of kids with their hands up, eager to ask questions. I answered as many as I could; I was starting to enjoy myself. But then the school captain, a student named Jack, asked me about the man I'd just spoken of so fondly in my talk, and I froze and felt myself thrown backwards into the emotion of memory. The thought of him still hit me squarely in the chest, even after all this time.

But really that made sense. He had shaped my life, and he was one of the major reasons I'd come to believe in the power of kindness in the first place. His name was Jim.

• • •

It was a Monday morning and I had just finished a rehab session in the pool with a physiotherapist. It had been gruelling, as you'd expect in the early stages of recovery. I swam to the edge of the pool, where I waited for some help to get out. My physio started to give me a hand, and I balanced awkwardly on the pool's edge—about the furthest thing from graceful that you could imagine.

One of the orderlies was waiting poolside with my wheelchair and a towel, and next to him was a young man—another inpatient on a tour during their induction. Our eyes locked as I looked up at him. It sounds like a cliché but seeing him almost took my breath away. He had boyish good looks: blue eyes that sent me into a trance, and thick, dark brown hair that in time I would find hard to run my fingers through.

I sensed how vulnerable he felt in the new environment of rehab from his shy smile, but I noticed as I introduced myself that his smile grew larger. I like to think that our meeting gave him a sense of comfort. For me, it was refreshing to have someone there who was similar to me in age.

Jim and I soon became inseparable. I learned that he had found himself in rehab after injuring himself in an obstacle race, falling very awkwardly and from a great height. He had fractured multiple parts of his spine and was also relearning how to walk and adjusting to his new normal. We had plenty in common—a love of sport, good humour and the beaches— and we found ways around our personalised rehab schedules to laugh together and banter with each other. I memorised Jim's schedule, and soon enough I found myself 'accidentally' running in to him—having finished a session of mine in the area I knew he would be in. Jim learned my schedule too, and quite often I'd find him lurking outside the treatment rooms when he knew I would be there.

One afternoon I caught him out: I saw him speaking on the phone right outside the room I was in, just loud enough for me to hear. As I edged towards the door, I saw him jump a little in his chair when his phone started ringing. I laughed when I realised that he had been pretending to be on the phone so that I would hear him. I never told him about that, but I took it as a sign that he liked spending time with me which I was thrilled with because I knew I had started having deeper feelings for him.

I'm not sure exactly when we realised that we wanted more than a friendship. If it wasn't love at first sight, it was pretty damn close. The first time we said it out loud was the first night Jim got caught in my room by one of the staff. We didn't get in trouble or anything like that, but we knew we were supposed to be in our designated areas for checks, so we felt a little mischievous. As Jim tidied himself up and hurried out the door, he looked back and casually said, 'Love you.' That was it. Not some grand moment like you see in movies, but it felt so genuine, like it was the most natural thing ever.

Because of where and how we met, whenever other patients or staff members saw us together, they always wore a sly smile. Looking back, it's easy to see why it made them happy: how often do people find love in a rehab centre?

From the very beginning, our relationship surprised me. Firstly, I never expected to find romance in a rehab centre as I was trying to overcome life-altering injuries. But I was also surprised by the way we were able to turn these life-changing experiences into something as deep and as special as what we had.

Jim was my first real boyfriend. Sure, I'd had a high-school crush that turned into something more, but nothing solid—I had always been too preoccupied with cricket and study. About three months into our relationship, I remember feeling grateful that I had broken my back—as if I hadn't, I would not have met him. I would not have experienced the magic that life can be when you are so deeply in love with the person you were born to spend the rest of your life with.

Jim had a way of making everyone feel welcome. It didn't matter if you were a cleaner or a brain surgeon—everyone was greeted with a warm smile and a friendly gesture. It was his beautiful and gentle soul and the deep, loving concern he had for everyone around him that made me fall in love with him in the first place. Anyone he spoke to was always made to feel like the most special person in the world. But if I had to pick just one thing about Jim that I loved the most, it was his humility.

Jim had an almost childlike innocence about him, and it was hard not to be drawn in by his charm and charisma. I loved watching him with Daisy—the two of us had become the three of us since I proudly introduced them. They shared stories and took turns making the cups of tea that we looked forward to every day. Daisy's health meant that she was often hard to understand, and many people—including staff—almost put her in the too-hard basket. Jim and I liked to make up for that by spending as much time as we could with her.

The more time Jim and I spent in the geriatric ward, the more people we met and stories we heard. And as we met war heroes and veterans, we were not only given a good dose of perspective but also a sense of gratitude for all those who had come before us. If we ever dared to feel sorry for ourselves and the situation we had found ourselves in, we only had to recall those who had literally gone to war for us, to allow us to be living in freedom. Many of these patients became very good friends to Jim and me, and soon our favourite thing to do—apart from planning our own future—was to spend time with the oldies.

When we weren't with Daisy or attending to our rehab programs, Jim and I had a lot of fun, sometimes joking about our injuries and disabilities but also testing each other out in the corridors with a pastime that became famous among the younger patients—wheelchair racing.

Most people wouldn't consider wheelchair racing a dangerous sport, but it was. We were brutal in our pursuit of winning those races, and looked forward to the thrill of the competition, especially as we knew we weren't supposed to be doing it in the first place. Some staff frowned upon it and would shut it down at every chance, but others turned a blind eye and gave us the chance to feel like regular people again. We took so much joy from these apparently insignificant moments in rehab—they represented an escape from the reality of our situation.

It's often said that you become your environment, and when you're in the grind of rehab for as long as we were, it's easy to adapt to the life you find there. It can quickly become consuming and you could easily forget about the career you'd had, the role you'd played in society or even how you fitted into your own family dynamic.

Fortunately, I was working part-time remotely in sports administration, and had friends and family who I saw regularly, meaning that I was always somewhat connected to the outside world. Jim's mum, Wendy, played that role for him, visiting every other week from the Gold Coast, keeping him connected to his family and life outside of rehab. I know how greatly he appreciated that, especially given the effort and expense Wendy incurred to get there as often as she could. For both of us, our connection to family gave us fresh perspective and a sense of gratitude, which helped keep us grounded.

It was different for many other patients. Some, for whatever reason, had very few visitors, or their injuries prevented them from working or studying. Their world became quite small, with only one thing to focus on.

When you're injured in a way that requires rehab, you can find yourself craving your old life and searching for small wins that wouldn't normally have meant much to you. It's a basic human need to have a sense of control over your life. In rehab, however, it's easy to become so fixated on your recovery that everything becomes a competition, either with yourself, as you try to beat your previous efforts, or with whoever else is in the room.

Jim wasn't one of those patients. Sure, he was driven, but only in the pursuit of a healthy and balanced recovery. At times, as I watched him master a new skill, I was in awe of how easy he made it look. He had always been active prior to his accident, and sport was something he enjoyed, so the fact that he took to his recovery well made a lot of sense. I wasn't so naturally gifted, though, and so I often found myself spending longer and longer in therapy rooms, trying 'just one more time' to get something right. I became quite competitive with myself.

Sundays were always a quieter day in rehab. They meant a day off from the exercise and therapies, and most patients applied for day passes if they had family and friends who could take them out and care for them. Jim and I usually had a day out of rehab, but every so often we stayed in. Depending on how the week had gone for you, it was also often a chance to catch up on any of the new skills you were trying to master.

On one rare Sunday that we both stayed back, we woke up, had a bite of breakfast and then I started making my way towards a treatment room, telling Jim I'd see him in a couple of hours. I was at a point in my recovery where I had started to regain some feeling in my leg, and I had been relearning how to balance myself for at least a few weeks. I finally felt like I was getting somewhere and having a quieter space to practise in, without the distraction of other patients, was quite helpful.

Time flew by, and before I knew it, it was lunchtime. I sent Jim a text to see where he was. I waited a while without a response, then my lunch arrived. As I ate, I called him but got no answer. *He must be working on his own rehab,* I thought.

It was just before three in the afternoon that I decided to track him down. I knew it would only be a matter of time before I ran into him somewhere, but I hadn't thought I would find him in the first place that I looked: with Daisy. I could hear the two of them laughing uncontrollably as I got out of the elevator and it was hard not to smile myself.

'What's so funny?' I asked as I entered the room. They let me in on the joke—something they had just watched on the TV show *M*A*S*H*. For a few minutes I felt like I was intruding on their time together, but soon I'd warmed myself into the flow of conversation. Jim and I stayed with Daisy until about four, and then went outside for some fresh air—knowing that soon enough it would be dinner, and we'd be preparing for a fresh week of rehab.

'What have you got this week?' he asked.

I rattled off the schedule that I had taken a peek at earlier that day. 'You?'

'I haven't actually had a look yet. Same old stuff, I reckon.'

For as much as we had in common, I was surprised by how little preparation Jim seemed to do when it came to his rehab schedule, yet it seemed easy for him to do. I felt like I had to carefully plan every moment of my rehab to get any gains.

'What did you get up to today?' I asked him.

'Hung out with Daisy!'

I smiled. 'The entire time?'

'Yeah, pretty much.'

I knew they couldn't have left the confines of Daisy's room, as she was too immobile at that point in her recovery. I loved that they enjoyed each other's company, but I was pretty sure that was the first time Jim had visited her without me there.

'What made you do that?' I asked him.

He looked at me, confused. 'What do you mean?' he asked.

Jim genuinely enjoyed her company, which shouldn't have come as a surprise to me. What did surprise me, though, was learning that his visits to Daisy were a welcome distraction for him from the grind of rehab. He'd had about all he could take of exercises that week, and he didn't want to think about his schedule or the week ahead. But after spending most of the day with Daisy and giving himself that mental break, he knew he could face the week ahead.

Jim's self-awareness impressed me. His comment next, though, really highlighted his humility.

'I couldn't do this without you or Daisy,' he said, looking me in the eye.

I haven't done a thing, I kept thinking, *and especially not today.*

'You both keep me on track,' Jim went on. 'I'm so glad we are all in this together.'

Humility, I understood in that moment, was not the absence of confidence. It was the desire to recognise the contribution of others, whichever way it comes to us.

Jim's humility drew people to him, and in that moment on that Sunday, I realised something important about him. His humility didn't make him feel like a lesser person. Acknowledging the support of others actually lifted him higher and gave him a greater sense of purpose. It was there in the way he always made Daisy feel like the most important person in the room, and in how, when faced with a choice between being right and being kind, he always chose kindness, whatever he had to give up to do so.

• • •

As I stood on the stage at the school in Goulburn, with my heart in my mouth, I tried to explain to the students everything that Jim was. The way he treated not only me but everyone around him with genuine care. I could see Jack, the school captain, listening closely. As I watched his young face light up with curiosity about the man I loved, I lost my composure. I wiped away the tears that had begun to form in my eyes, a little embarrassed that after all I'd been through, it was a school hall full of kids that had brought me undone.

As I stepped away from the microphone to regather myself, Jack sprang to his feet and gave me a hug. My emotions were running away from me, and the fact that this young man had taken the initiative to comfort me—exactly as Jim would have done—just about tipped me over the edge.

What happened next completely floored me. Jack gently eased the microphone out of my hand and stepped forward to address the students in the hall. He told the room how much my story had resonated with him, as a young athlete who felt the pressure of achieving his sporting goals. He spoke up in front of all his peers about his vulnerability. It was a remarkable moment, and I felt like I'd made a true and tangible connection—and the other kids clearly thought so too, as it prompted many to stand up and share their own experiences of hardship and loss.

By the time the bell rang, the feeling in the room was one of openness and empathy. As I stood chatting to the line of students who wanted to thank me, I was amazed by their thoughtfulness. In the end the teachers had to usher the kids off to their next classes.

As I walked away from the school, looking out for the man who'd offered to drive me to my next destination, you couldn't wipe the smile off my face.

• • •

I'd arranged to meet Damian at a park in Goulburn, just down the road from the school. I had no idea who he was: a friend of his who had heard about my journey had passed on my details to him after learning that I needed a ride.

As I waited by the empty oval on a deserted street corner, a hint of nervousness crept through me. What was I thinking, accepting a lift from a man I'd never met, a man who could have any kind of shady past or agenda? If one of the students I'd just spent my morning with had been planning to get into a car with someone they didn't know, I'd have told them unequivocally not to. In fact, some of the teachers had raised their eyebrows as I'd explained where I was going next—as if this were a horror story waiting to happen.

I swallowed. I would see what this guy looked like when he pulled up, I told myself, then make my decision. I hated the idea of judging someone by their appearance, but I also needed to put my safety first. This journey was crazy enough as it was.

A minute later, a dark blue sedan stopped beside me and a man wearing casual shorts and a T-shirt opened the door. 'Kath?' he asked expectantly.

'Yes, that's me,' I said, and I walked around the car to shake his hand.

'Damian. Nice to meet you,' he replied. 'Shall we get going? I've got school pickup back in Shellharbour this afternoon.'

He smiled politely and I made my decision. This man had just driven two hours to give me a lift. Surely that counted for a lot.

I slipped into the passenger seat and rested my backpack at my feet. 'Thanks so much for doing this,' I said as Damian pulled the car out from the kerb.

'No problem. Kelly said you needed a lift. Where are you off to?'

I gave him a confused look. 'Wait, you don't know what I'm doing?'

Damian returned an equally baffled glance. 'Something in Shellharbour?'

I couldn't suppress a smile, and for the next two hours Damo and I just talked. He was a former real estate agent who'd lived a fast-paced life for twenty years. Two years earlier, the stress of that lifestyle had got the better of him and he had relocated from Sydney to Shellharbour to escape the fast-paced rat race of city life in Sydney. He made this decision for his health and wellbeing and that of his family.

Damo was honest about his situation, and as we talked about the power of vulnerability and sharing, I couldn't help but think how brave he was. Suddenly I was thinking of Jim again.

• • •

Amid the daily grind, rehab felt like it was passing by very slowly, but the reality of our situation was that both Jim and I were doing very well, and our physical recoveries were ahead of schedule. I think we could both put that down to the support we were able to provide each other, but also to the fact that we had started dreaming of our life together after rehab. Dreams like four kids—three boys and a girl, just like in my family—a home in Broadwater, on the Gold Coast, pet turtles and a dog named Saf.

After eight months of rehab, I started to regain some normality in my life. My injuries were nowhere near being recovered entirely, but it was now safe enough for me to regain some independence at home and begin to go to work part-time again, visiting rehab three mornings each week for general check-ups and to ensure everything stayed on track.

The biggest challenge I had, and still have, is the numb left leg that I continue to live with from the kneecap down. But aside from a few falls here and there in that initial stage of recovery, I was doing pretty well, especially considering what my original prognosis had been.

As Jim had sustained his injuries a little while after me, he would be an inpatient for a little while longer. It was hard to be away from each other, especially as we had spent the fundamental months of our relationship in that environment. I knew how lonely rehab could feel when you were there by yourself, so I made a point of visiting any chance I could, while also trying to focus on regaining my independence in the workplace and back at home. I knew that would be a big help for both Jim and me as we planned for his release.

Visiting Jim on his last day of rehab felt like one of the more rewarding experiences of my life at the time. As the time drew closer, we had crossed off days on the calendar with excitement. We had looked forward to this moment for what felt like an eternity—a day when all the dreams that we had been dreaming were about to come true.

That night Jim passed away.

My Jim. The strongest and kindest man I had ever known was now a memory. A man who would smile with his teeth. A smile so big that it lit up any room. A man whose blue eyes used to pop when he wore the shirt that he had on during our first date. A man who had scars on his back that matched mine. Scars that were three of my fingers long but only two and a half of his.

Jim would never smile again. I would never see those beautiful blue eyes again. He was gone, and not a day has passed that I haven't thought how I would give everything just to see him one more time. To hold him, and tell him that I can see the pain behind his beautiful smile, and that I am here. That I will always be here, and that I will show up and fight for him every single day.

Suddenly, I had lost what felt like everything. The man who was my future—who I had dreamed all these dreams with—had vanished in front of my eyes. Not one part of me saw it coming, and the torment that followed was something I wouldn't wish upon anyone.

What I have come to understand about suicide in the ten years since Jim passed is that we can never truly understand what another person is feeling. I had to learn to accept that, for Jim, the pain of dying was less than the pain he was experiencing in being alive. Every part of me wishes that I had known. I don't mean to say that I could have prevented his death, but I wish he had known that he wasn't alone in his struggle.

I have spent countless hours racking my brain, searching for clues and warning signs that I missed. But I know that Jim would not wish mental torment for me. I know that he loved me, just as I do him. Perhaps he loved me so much that he wanted to protect me from his pain. I will never truly know.

I do know that I love him so much that I accept his choice, despite the deep sadness I feel for what could have been, and without judgement. And my choice to live my life with our shared values of kindness, humour and humility is how I will continue his legacy.

I hit rock bottom ten months after Jim's passing, when I had a complete emotional breakdown. It was ugly—I remember struggling to breathe at certain points. Looking back now, I don't remember too much of it. Most of that period blends into one big ball of grief that I spent the next few years trying to forget.

Grief has a funny way of finding you, though, even when you push it as far down as I did in the immediate aftermath of Jim's death. Sometimes a smell or a song on the radio would send me down a rabbit hole of memories. I learned the hard way that we can't hide from grief—we simply have to feel it. Although I tried hard to forget about my feelings, they would surface at times that surprised me. And when they hit me, rather than dealing with them, I would run.

In a literal sense, I found an escape in exercise, even with the disabilities I now lived with. In a metaphorical sense, I ran as far away from my grief as I could by avoiding conversations that reminded me of rehab. I'd change radio stations if a song

KINDNESS

reminded me of Jim, and I'd wake myself up before encounter-
ing a nightmare that had become a regular occurrence. I later
learned this was a symptom of the post-traumatic stress disorder
(PTSD) that I had been struggling with since his passing.

• • •

At the time I shared all of this with Damo in the car, it was
close to the four-year anniversary of Jim's passing. We looked
at each other for a few moments and I realised that Damo
had pulled over to the side of the road so he could give his
full attention to what I was telling him. In what I can only
describe as one of the most beautiful moments of my life,
he then leaned over and hugged me with his big arms.

This beautiful, strong man held me in his arms as I sobbed
uncontrollably. He didn't hurry me along in my tears—he had
all the time in the world for me. I will never forget his care
for me in that moment. I will never forget his kindness towards
me, and what that moment meant to me as a person. I think
it was the first time that I grieved for Jim properly. Damo
doesn't even know that he did this for me. I only wish he and
Jim had met. They would have been really good friends.

Damo's humility, like Jim's, stood out to me. He was a busy
dad, yet he had chosen to come and pick me up for a four-hour

round trip. He was a man who had the courage to be vulnerable and accepting of his own fears and insecurities. A man who wasn't too proud to leave behind his successful career in search of better health. A man who was not too important to take time out of his day for me, a stranger.

Damo was fully present in our moments together, as if there was nowhere in the world that it was more important for him to be. I had his full attention. He knew when to ask for help in his own life, with his own health struggles. He had learned these skills through life's ups and downs. And as he shared more about himself with me, and I offered something in return by describing my own experiences, he was receptive to that feedback, no doubt taking from it what he could.

That's what makes people with humility special. They aren't simply self-deprecating, like some might think. They practise enough self-awareness to know their own strengths and weaknesses; it's their humility that enables them to grow.

Like all the people I'd connected with on my journey to date, Damo would never again be a stranger to me. Since returning from my journey, I have met his whole family. He and my brother sometimes go fishing together, and I've spoken at one of his daughters' schools as part of the Kindness Factory's programs. Damo is always one of the first among our 3.5-million-strong community to put his hand up to help when someone is in need.

I have encountered many people whose stories I could have used to illustrate what humility means to me. But as I began exploring them, I realised that humility isn't one single thing. It's the little things that we do each day that make humility powerful.

It's interesting to be writing about humility, given that I've started a global movement that encourages people to share their acts of kindness. Some might argue that that's the opposite of humility. I disagree. Humility isn't defined by the absence of an audience. It takes tremendous courage and vulnerability to share such things, in my opinion. It is the recognition of your own shortcomings and the desire to recognise the contributions of others that makes humility so very special and warm.

Some of the most well-known athletes in the world are often admired most for their humility. To be the best, they obviously have a high level of confidence to get to the heights that they have reached. So humility isn't necessarily self-deprecating like some people may think: it's actually about acknowledging our shared humanity, and being about to see the bigger picture, beyond the sporting field or the office board room.

Gratitude

I stood on the footpath in front of Joe and Leanne's place in Shellharbour feeling exhausted, but also a lot lighter. It was midafternoon and warm, which was surprising given I could hear the waves crashing against the rocks not too far away. I double-checked I had the right address, waved Damo off and walked hesitantly up the carefully maintained front path.

Joe and Leanne had offered to put me up for as long as I needed. I also had an offer from the homeless shelter nearby their home: they had invited me to help for the day in exchange for a meal and a yarn with some of their regulars. After doing some checks, I figured out that I had a few common connections with Joe and Leanne from when they had lived in Sydney, which put my mind at ease.

I knocked with more confidence than I was feeling, but as soon as Leanne opened the door, I felt a wave of relief. I felt safe—I would be able to rest.

Joe and Leanne had been married for the best part of 30 years. Some of their adult children lived close by in Shellharbour and some lived in Sydney. As I walked into the house, I caught the scent of a freshly caught fish baking in the oven. Leanne introduced me to Joe, who had been out in his boat and caught our dinner. Leanne was in the middle of cutting up the potatoes for some home-made chips to go along with it. They seemed like a great team.

I was feeling drained—my talk at the school had been quite heavy, and then the car ride with Damo had exhausted me emotionally—and I think this was pretty obvious to Joe and Leanne. I showered and changed into my spare set of clothes, then rested on the lounge. I had offered to help set the table for dinner but had been refused by my hosts. After dinner, though, I did manage to help with the dishes. Then I asked if either of them would mind if I had an early night, and I was met with a smile and goodnight hug.

Joe and Leanne were perfect hosts for me in that moment, putting their curiosity for me and my journey aside and letting me get an early night. It was a simple gesture, but one that I appreciated enormously.

In bed in one of the spare rooms of their home, I kept thinking about the day I'd just had. This journey was changing my life in so many ways. I couldn't help but feel immense gratitude to be sleeping in a warm bed with a roof over my head. Especially considering where I was going the next day.

I woke to the smell of eggs cooking, and as I showered and started mentally preparing for my day ahead, I could hear Joe bidding Leanne farewell. They were a wonderful couple in love, which was so refreshing to see.

I told Leanne I was planning to walk to Kiama that day, which made her giggle—it turned out I had miscalculated the distance and it would take me a couple of hours to get to the hall where I would be serving the homeless community lunch. Leanne told me she had a few errands to run, and we wanted to spend a few more moments together anyway, so she gave me a ride into town. There we said our goodbyes and promised to stay in touch.

At the hall I was recognised by the head volunteer and her daughter, who were to help me find my way around the kitchen for my shift, in exchange for a meal and the chance to meet some new friends—the people we would be serving. Once the last guest had filled their plate, it was time for me to get to know a few of the folks who had joined us.

Spending time with these people who were doing it tough was fascinating. Each of them had a story of significant trauma and adversity that was hard to comprehend. A lot of what they were telling me resonated with my own experience—the pain they felt and the hardship they had been through. I realised, though, how very lucky I was to be doing what I was.

Back when I set out on this trip, I had hoped it would help me learn about something deeper than myself, perhaps so I could understand my adversities a little better. And now, as I sat there talking to one of my new friends, a small piece of my life started to make more sense.

I saw now that one of the main things that had allowed me to overcome adversity was my incredible support network. I simply would not be the person I am today without them— all those people who have chosen, time and time again, to show up for me. In the good moments, sure, but also in the tough moments when no one knows what to say or how to be, especially through my periods of trauma and grief.

Those people who showed up for me regardless of the struggle I was in, and who sat with me in my pain, are the people I hold closest to my heart. And there are so many of them— too many to mention. I wouldn't be half the person I am without their love and support. Somehow, it took meeting this community of homeless people to remind me of how very lucky I was to have had their unwavering support, even at my lowest moment.

• • •

After Jim's passing, when I was truly at rock bottom, I found a few important things there. First, the realisation that things couldn't possibly be tougher than they were in those moments. But I also discovered that up was the only direction that made sense to me now, since I couldn't get any lower.

After a routine check-up at the rehab centre one day about ten months after Jim's death, I found myself walking past his old room. A wave of grief and trauma hit me like a tonne of bricks. I was overwhelmed in that moment by so many emotions: fear, deep sadness, regret, and a yearning I didn't know was possible. So my rock bottom moment involved four nurses pinning me down and sedating me after I lost control of myself in that moment of grief.

It wasn't pretty. I wasn't a risk to anyone else, but I guess I posed a danger to myself. My grief had overtaken my brain and body, and the only way I could express it was a combination of running into walls and holding my head as if it were about to explode. I simply could not process so many emotions and feelings at once amid this wave of trauma triggered by Jim's old room.

When I woke from the sedation, I felt a haze of confusion, almost like a severe hangover. My head was throbbing and I felt light-headed and dizzy. But I also felt a deep sense of shame.

My stirring attracted the attention of the nurses, who hurried over to me to give what they thought would be received as reassuring words: 'Kath, everything is okay. You're going to be okay. You've been through a lot. What you have been through is not normal, but your response to it is.'

Hindsight is a wonderful thing, and as I look back now, I know these words were intended in the right way—to reassure me that I was in good hands and was going to get the help that I needed. But all I could think at the time was that if this was what 'normal' felt like, then 'normal' wasn't for me.

I did what I had to do—showered, brushed my hair and cleaned my teeth—and then I grabbed a coffee, which helped me stabilise myself as much as possible in the next few hours. Then I decided that enough was enough: it was time for me to take control of my life again and stop feeling sorry for myself.

I knew in my gut that the place for me to start again was on the Gold Coast. The place where Jim and I had planned to start our life together. I left rehab that day, booked a taxi home, packed a backpack and went to book a taxi to the airport. As I was about to hit book, I heard my mum arriving, which was surprising: it was just past lunchtime and she should have been at work. It took her all of a few seconds to realise that I wasn't okay; when she asked me how I was doing, I burst into tears.

I told her my plan—that I needed to get to the Gold Coast to do a bit of soul searching. I could tell that she was worried about me, but she was also incredibly supportive and agreed to drive me to the airport. I was out of words by this point; I switched the radio to an FM station and turned the volume up. Mum and I sat in silence for most of the drive, just listening to the music.

We hugged tight at the airport and I promised her I'd be safe, but from the look on her face, I knew she'd be worried sick the entire time I was away. I hated seeing her and the rest of my family and friends worry, but I also knew that I needed to prioritise myself and give myself what I felt I needed. The next time Mum picked me up from the airport she told me she had kept the radio station on that same FM channel the entire time I was away: it was a way for her to feel connected to me. *There must be a million little things that our parents do for us out of love even when we aren't aware of it,* I thought.

After saying goodbye to Mum, I sat on the plane jetting towards the Gold Coast, and started to feel a weight lift off my shoulders. This was the first time in my life, adversity or not, that I had prioritised my emotions and my mental health. It was something that I needed to do, and something I should have done much sooner.

After we touched down, I was soon on the freeway towards Jim's mum's place. I adored Wendy—she had treated me like her own daughter when Jim and I were together. But, absorbed by my own grief, I had practically ignored her in the ten months leading up to this day.

I got out of the car and hurried towards Wendy's home as if it held the oxygen that I needed to breathe again. When she opened the door, I almost fell into her arms. There were so many things that I had planned to say: 'sorry' was the first among them. Sorry for the loss that she had endured. Sorry for ignoring the grief that she, as a mother, must have felt at losing her only son. And sorry that I had not shared in that grief with her, as we could have.

But none of those sorrys made it out of my mouth. Wendy knew I was sorry. I didn't need to say it and she didn't need to hear it. She needed to hold me, and I needed to hold her. Words weren't necessary in that moment: our embrace said all that needed saying.

We sat in the hallway of her home for hours, holding each other's pain, and eventually we both realised that night-time had fallen. We had plenty of time in the coming weeks to catch up and heal together, so we both put ourselves to bed.

It felt like home being back with Wendy. This was the place I needed to be to rediscover what my life could become.

Rock bottom became a foundation on which I could start to build the rest of my life. And that realisation gave me hope.

About a week into my stay on the Gold Coast, the dial started to shift when I truly started to tap in to the power of gratitude. I walked into the living room one morning to find the house silent: Wendy had gone out to grab some groceries, and had left a note to let me know. Next to it on the coffee table was a blank piece of lined paper and a pen.

As I sat on the lounge staring at that piece of paper, I began to compile a list in my mind of all the people who had shown up for me in my life—especially those who had shown up for me in the past year, when I'd been incapable of doing the same in return. Wendy was high up the list, but there were also family and friends, doctors and physios. Almost without thinking, I picked up the pen and starting writing down their names. Before I knew it, there were 30 names on the piece of paper.

I knew each of those 30 people had my back—they had got me through some of the most challenging experiences life could throw at anyone. I imagined them in a room together and felt a wave of gratitude flow through me. Thirty people was a lot, and this list was just off the top of my head. I felt like I was being given the answer to a quiz question that had been puzzling me—and it turned out I'd known the answer all along.

I opened my phone and, again without giving it too much thought, started calling everyone on the list to thank them.

The first person I rang was one of the doctors who had saved my leg, who had taken a vested interest in my recovery. He must have seen my name flash up on his screen when I called because he immediately picked up and said, 'Oh my gosh, Kath, what have you done? What have you broken? How can I help?'

'Hi, Doc, everything's okay, I'm okay. Doc, I'm just calling to say thanks. Thanks for helping me in the way that you have, and for always going above and beyond for me. I really appreciate it.'

There was silence for a few seconds, then finally he responded. 'Kath, you don't have to thank me. Everything I have done for you has been an absolute privilege, and I am so proud to have played a small part in your life to date. Thanks for the call—and before you hang up, I want you to know that I am so proud of the person you are.'

I went on to call every person on that list, each of whom gave a similar response. A lot of tears were shared, and a lot of laughs. I put the bulk of my long-term emotional recovery down to those three hours that I spent calling those people. It wasn't profound in the moment—my life and experiences didn't suddenly all make sense to me—but it helped me recognise how lucky I was to have people in my life who were always so generous in their support of me.

Gratitude is powerful. And the best thing about it is that you don't have to wait for adversity to strike before you embrace it. Since that day back in late 2013, I haven't stopped embracing it. It is without doubt one of the most powerful ingredients for resilience that we humans have.

Gratitude excludes no one—we all have something to be grateful for. It can be for the people we share our lives with, or it can be for what we see and do every single day. It might be for your support networks, or for someone in the street who smiles at you, or for experiences you've had. There is always a reason to be grateful. Gratitude helps give us perspective, and a greater capacity for kindness towards ourselves and others.

I genuinely believe that the best gift you can give another is to thank them for being in your life. When I share the power of gratitude with audiences around the world now, I set them a challenge.

'Think of your favourite person in the world,' I say. 'It might be your spouse, your child or your best friend. It's their birthday coming up and you want to get them a gift that you know they will just love. So you go to a store, you pick out the gift, you pay for it and then you wrap it up. You might even put a bow on it. You take it home and then you throw it in the cupboard and never give it to them. It's a complete waste.

'The same thing can be said about gratitude. Feeling it for someone and not telling them is a waste. Who are you grateful for? Have you told them? If yes, great. If not, why not?'

I guarantee you that gratitude is the best gift you can ever give that person. And it will only strengthen the bond you have with them. There's no greater act of kindness than that.

• • •

Once lunch at the shelter had finished and the guests had started to depart, I helped the volunteers with the dishes and started mopping the floor. As I worked my way towards the entry doors, I noticed that one of the guests from lunch was sitting there looking out to the waterfront of Kiama.

I said g'day and asked if everything was okay. His name was Patrick, but I hadn't had the chance to sit with him during lunch like I had with most of the others. I let Patrick know that when I'd finished the clean-up with the other volunteers, I'd enjoy sitting with him if he had a few moments.

When I farewelled the volunteers, they handed me a package of food for my bag. I didn't know where my next meal was coming from, and I wasn't keen to tap into the cash I'd being collecting as my journey continued. I didn't have a lot, but it would be enough to get me out of trouble for a night or two if I needed it. I was also feeling pretty well fed—hunger hadn't bothered me at all. (The irony of saying this as I write about the community I had just served that day is not lost on me. I was well aware what a privilege this journey had been to date.)

As I sat with Patrick and heard his story, I had to take a few deep breaths at times. Patrick was a two-time cancer survivor who had given away all of his money to various cancer charities instead of saving it for himself. He had done this because he felt such gratitude for the organisations that had supported him through his recovery, and because he didn't want others to suffer as he had. He wasn't necessarily homeless, but the money he earned only covered his rent plus medical bills and essentials, so meals like this were needed and always welcome. Patrick wore his favourite AFL team's cap—he was a Carlton supporter through and through—and I sensed that watching the Blues play gave him hope and something to look forward to every week of the season. The more I learned about Patrick, the more admiration I felt for him.

Eventually I told Patrick that I had to get to the train station and asked for directions. He walked me there, and as we were saying goodbye, I asked him where home was. As it happened, it was on the way to where I was going, but he was planning to walk the four kilometres to save himself the train fare. The least I could do for Patrick in that moment was pay for a train ticket for him. I knew that the people who had so generously given me donations would welcome me spending this small amount on someone like Patrick. It made me smile that I could do that for him. And it also meant that we could spend some more time together.

As we waited for our train to arrive, I had my very own South Coast tour guide. And so I heard a complete history of the South Coast from one of its finest residents, as Patrick took me through the stories of his mates, some of whom lived rough and others who didn't.

Patrick wasn't a flashy man. He'd lived a more affluent life in the past, but he didn't necessarily miss his old lifestyle. He was grateful for everything he had, and for the fact that he was here to see another day. After surviving cancer twice, he knew that each and every day was a gift.

The lesson in gratitude I took that day was a gift for which, appropriately enough, I was grateful. When I let Patrick know this, he simply smiled and wished me well on my journey, wherever it took me next.

Mindfulness

In the reception area of the Novotel hotel in Wollongong, Carly embraced me so tightly it was almost a headlock. As we held each other tight, I felt relief settle over me. It was close to two weeks since I had left my home, and I had stayed with two families after saying goodbye to Patrick. Now I was standing here surrounded by the familiarity of Carly's warmth and love, and familiarity was something that I had been longing for since I'd set out on this journey.

It had been a while since I'd seen Carly, and it was pure luck that brought us together now. Earlier that day, I had appeared on the local radio station, Wave FM, with one of their corporate sponsors, Novotel, offering me a free night by the beach. Carly lived in the area and heard the broadcast, and she shot me a text to see if I had some time to catch up.

It was interesting to hear her feedback about the segment itself. While most media interviews I'd done had been about my story, both past and the present, today I was asked about mental health. I realised from some of the callers' questions that my journey to date had started to resonate with a lot of people, who were thanking me for being so open in sharing my experiences with them. It appeared that my story was giving people hope, which surprised me but also made me feel good to think that people were being impacted in this way; challenging the stigma that sometimes comes with sharing our inner battles and consequently, help-seeking behaviours.

As Carly and I sat in the hotel courtyard looking out to the ocean, I shouted her a drink and we reminisced on our friendship. We met as thirteen-year-olds playing cricket, and we went on to undertake tertiary studies together across various sports diplomas. Our bond, forged through cricket, extended into our social lives. Soon enough we began spending more and more time together, skipping classes and dodging the responsibilities of young adults. We loved playing cricket and always aspired to higher honours, but we never took it too seriously.

Carly played for Bankstown in Sydney grade cricket in our teenage and young adult years, while I played for St George-Sutherland. Since we were close, I introduced her to two of my teammates, and she introduced me to two of hers. Add in the English international players that we each had in our teams, and there were eight of us mates who spent at least two great summers together. I can't remember a more carefree or relaxed period of my life. Thinking back to that time now, I wished I had savoured those moments more.

Hindsight can be destructive: we wish we had done more, realised something or seen a different point of view. We can be hard on ourselves. But in this instance, hindsight helped me understand something important. Friendship had always given me the strongest platform for mindfulness. I am my truest self and I am most present and at ease when I'm in the company of those I care about the most.

Mindfulness is often linked to 'Zen master' stereotypes, but I don't think it has to be that way. And we don't need expensive apps on our phones either to help us clear our minds and be present in the moment. That's not to say there's anything wrong with using mindfulness apps, but we can think more broadly about what true mindfulness can be.

My brother, Grant, for example, could spend entire days fishing. His partner often sends him down to the nearest fishing spot if she senses he is stressed. I've always hated fishing, but when I asked him what he loves about it, he says that's when his mind is the quietest. I've known professional athletes who say riding their bike does the same thing for them. My best friend is most present when she's cooking, and my nephew loves to dig holes.

For me, it's about friendship. True friendship is one of the best ways for me to stay in the moment, and that's how I practise mindfulness.

The longer Carly and I chatted, the funnier the stories got. We reminisced about the days we'd skipped classes—to no one's detriment but our own—the nights out we'd enjoyed on cricket tours, the stories from the dance floor. All of it was young, innocent and fun, which was the furthest thing from what my life had been in a long time.

I hadn't checked my phone once the entire night, I realised when I went back to my hotel room, and I had no regrets about that. In fact, it felt very similar to when I was first introduced to mindfulness, with Wendy up on the Gold Coast.

• • •

The line between okay and not okay is sometimes a fine one for me, considering the adversities I have been through. The moments that led me to find myself on the Gold Coast with Wendy were the toughest of my life to date but by the end of that three-week trip I had started to feel more like my healthier and happier self.

I put this down to a few things. Not the least of them was the start I'd made in reconnecting with the people in my life who meant the most to me—I was looking forward to seeing them in person again when I came back to Sydney. But I would be with Wendy for the next week or so, and I was determined to make that time as meaningful as I could.

On one of the last mornings together that week, we enjoyed the warmth of a coffee and watched the sun rise together while looking out at the gentle waves of Broadbeach. As we sat and watched the water, time seemed to pass without much urgency.

When I went to Wendy's home, I hadn't planned how long I would stay, and I was starting to miss my family and friends. I felt ready to head home. I started to get restless. The rock I was perched on was becoming uncomfortable, and I remember thinking that we should get going—we probably had somewhere to be. I stood up, feeling pins and needles as the blood rushed back into my legs.

Wendy didn't flinch when I stood up; she continued to watch the horizon with a serene look on her face. I waited a moment for her to notice me standing, wanting to ask her what we should do next.

Then, as I hopped from foot to foot to get some feeling back, I realised that we actually had nowhere to be. Why had I stood up in the first place? Why was I uncomfortable with the idea of 'wasting' more of our day, now that the sun had risen? I shook my head and sat back down, trying to summon the sense of peace I'd felt just moments earlier. And as I did so, I realised something.

As a young adult, I had never afforded myself the opportunity to simply *be*. Throughout my life until that point, in both good moments and bad, I had always been in a hurry. If I wasn't at school then I was at cricket training, or doing homework or chores set by Mum and Dad, and then, as I transitioned into life as a young adult, those responsibilities became playing cricket professionally, holding down a part-time job and studying. I always felt like I was running on a hamster wheel, as if I had to be somewhere else, always looking towards the next thing—the complete opposite of mindfulness and being present.

At that moment, though, sitting on that rock and staring out at the water with Wendy, it felt like the first time in my life that I had stopped and taken the moment for what it was, without thinking about the next challenge I was racing towards.

We sat there for another two hours, and I felt a clarity that I had been craving for a long time, perhaps my whole life. Everything that had seemed so daunting until that moment was now much lighter. The emotional processing that I was yet to do—the fact that I was 24 and without a job, having resigned from my part-time role to focus on my recovery, and that I had no real life direction suddenly felt more like a relief than a source of stress. It was an incredible shift in perspective, and one that I was lucky enough to experience without the pressure of needing to rush into anything, thanks to the incredible emotional and financial support of my family and friends. I was suddenly curious about my life and began thinking about what it could be, rather than focusing on all the adversities I had crawled through until that point.

With this shift in perspective, I found something important—hope. I'd travelled to the Gold Coast feeling lost, afraid and vulnerable, but I was suddenly looking forward to the future and all it could be. I knew it would be different from anything I had known before.

As she drove me to the airport for my flight home to Sydney, Wendy made a pact with me to stay in touch at least once a week. It was important to me to stay true to that pact, and I always looked forward to speaking to Wendy on the phone, even though we mostly chatted about nothing in particular. It was good to have that time each week with someone who knew what I'd been through, and who reminded me to stay in the moment and not let the busyness of life overwhelm me.

Back at home, I began finding my feet again in the faster pace of Sydney. I applied for a job at both Coles and Woolworths as a night-shift shelf packer, but was knocked back by each of them due to my back injury. Normally that rejection would have sunk me down again, but I had confidence I'd find something soon enough. One day soon after, a former boss of mine, who I had done some ad hoc part-time work for in the past, let me know that he had a job going in his operations team at Cricket NSW.

As I considered applying for the role, I wondered if all my new-found peace would vanish if I went back into an old environment, but it was the best option I had. Part of me was excited to see old friends and colleagues again, and the other part of me worried whether I might find it tough to be in that training environment again, but as support staff rather than as a player. I'd be close to my teammates again, which was a positive, but really I longed to be back on the pitch. As I went through the interview process and was offered the job, I still wasn't quite sure what I should do, so I asked them for a few days to consider everything.

The start of a new cricket season was approaching, and I told myself that not playing cricket anymore would at least give me the chance to enjoy some summer weekends at the beach. I'd spent more than half my life playing cricket in summer, and the thought of doing something different started to excite me.

On the first weekend of spring, however, reality hit me like a brick to the face. I planned to head to the beach at Cronulla to enjoy a burst of good weather, but as I started packing towels and hats into my car, I felt lost and alone. As I drove towards

Cronulla, my eyes filled with tears as I realised that the beach wouldn't be anywhere near as fun without my friends there to enjoy it with me. The majority of them were out on the cricket field, chasing the dreams that were still a possibility for them, while I was crying in my car. It was a sobering moment.

I parked my car at Cronulla, and decided that a quick dip in the ocean would make me feel better. As I swam and enjoyed the surf, I came to understand two things:

1. I loved cricket, and if I couldn't play it, then the next best thing was to work in it somehow. At least then I'd be in a cricketing environment once again.
2. The good things in my life were only truly meaningful to me when I could share them with friends and those who I cared about.

My new employers were patient about my return to work, and ensured that I only started in the role when I was ready. Even so, my palms were sweaty on my steering wheel as I sat in bumper-to-bumper traffic on the way to Cricket NSW's headquarters on day one. I was met by the acting HR manager and given a tour, where I bumped into more and more familiar faces and was shown to my desk.

Then I was introduced to a woman called Justine Whipper— known as 'Whip' by all in the office. She was responsible for the wellbeing and career development of all the players, and she was perfect in that role. My nervousness quickly melted away. The more I've come to know Whip, the more I understand that this was due to her kind, compassionate, humble and vulnerable nature. She made me feel at ease as I immersed myself in what was my first real job.

The Cricket NSW staff welcomed me back as though I had never left—which was both good and bad. Sometimes I felt a pressure to distance myself from the playing group so I wasn't a distraction, but most of the players were respectful towards me and my new role, which helped a lot. There was the occasional invitation to lunch, which I always tried to get out of. I wanted to maintain a professional distance from the playing group, but I had also found that a lot of people really had no idea what to say to someone who had endured what I had. In many ways I found it less awkward to stick to my new colleagues.

With Whip I had a blank canvas. I didn't want to hide my past from her, but not seeing constant sympathy in her eyes and her smile when we spoke was rare for me at that time. Gradually we became closer, and soon enough I was a regular in her office on a Friday afternoon, where we'd talk about all things, big and small, that went on around the office. We had very different roles, but both involved an element of service to the playing group, and I regularly used that as an excuse to drop in on her.

The thing I love most about Whip is that she doesn't sweat the small stuff, and she's not afraid to laugh at herself either. I am quite often easily distracted, especially if I'm not interested in the task at hand. I've been that way since I was a child. When I was with Whip, I was always 100 per cent engaged, whether we were working or just enjoying lunch or a walk in the park.

I put this down to a few things. Firstly, when you have someone in your life whom you admire that much, it's hard not to want to take in everything about them, which made being present easier for me—I was hanging on every word she said. Secondly, Whip's great sense of humour gave me permission to laugh, which again kept me present. And thirdly, Whip really cared. About everyone. And when you're in the presence of someone who cares that much, it's hard not to be grateful and stay in the moment.

Whip was the friend and colleague I needed at that point in my recovery. She came into my life without judgement or any reminders of my past—which is ironic, because the more time we spent together and the more I got to know her, the more she reminded me of Wendy and the homely feeling she had recently given me. In Whip's presence I could just be who I was, without carrying the emotion of my past. I think that's something we all need at certain points in our lives.

There's nothing more important in my life than friendship, and when I consider all that Whip is to me, I'd say that she changed my life. She was the breath of fresh air I needed to give me the clarity to simply just be me. For the first time in a long time, I felt hope for my future. I didn't know what the coming months and years would bring, but I was determined to be open to them.

Meeting Whip taught me that you always have room for one more friend in your life. After I finished high school, I was quickly so busy with training and part-time work that I told myself I didn't need to make any new friends on campus. *You don't have enough time for new friends—plus, you have enough friends in your life to be happy,* I said to myself as I ran off to my next training or study session. I now regret not taking the time to get to know some of the other students.

You may not have met your Whip yet—that person who makes it all make sense, and who gives you the clarity you need to live your life as the person you are, not the person that you were or that everyone thinks that you should be. And that's another great reason to be open to new friendships.

No one is immune to adversity. To me, a friend is someone who reminds you to feel alive even when living has become difficult. In my darkest hours, I have been so fortunate in that friends have never been far away. I owe my life to my friends—they are all gifts to my world, and I am lucky to have every one of them.

When I was struggling the most, I often told myself that I owed it to my friends to push on, and so that's what I did. I'd imagine the days we would have together, laughing at absolutely nothing at all, not being able to stop and then laughing some more. Being truly present in each other's company without a care in the world.

. . .

When I set out on my kindness journey, it was not lost on me that it was all about connecting with strangers—but it also made me realise just how important my friends are to me. They will always contribute hugely to me being the best version of myself. Writing about it right now has made me realise that spending time with close friends and with strangers is great for me, and keeps me well balanced.

Mindfulness is many things to many people, and I think it's important to put your own spin on it. To me, mindfulness is a form of self-kindness; it may be that to you too. Perhaps it's the oxygen mask that we put on ourselves before we help others. Because we can't be truly kind to others if we haven't first been kind to ourselves.

Positivity

I'd been flown to Melbourne by a man called George. That was all I knew about him after a brief conversation on the phone while I was in Shellharbour. He had no social media, so I couldn't even do an online 'stalk' in the leadup, as I had done with most of the people I was meeting. He sounded nice enough on the phone, offering to pay for my plane fare to Melbourne if I had accommodation options. His only request was that we meet for a coffee at some point.

I'd made a point of trusting my gut on this journey, and something drew me towards the friendly stillness in George's voice. I also had a couple of hundred offers from other people in Melbourne, so it wasn't the hardest decision to head south. I did, however, find it curious that someone was paying for my entire airfare just to have a coffee with me.

A friend's friend, Beth, had reached out to offer me a meal at the cafe she owned in Heidelberg Heights, and another friend of a friend had offered to let me stay in their apartment while they were interstate travelling. I landed in the afternoon, so I locked in the apartment for the first night and the cafe for the following day. But by the time I had landed, the apartment offer had fallen through, so I was immediately on the back foot.

In the arrivals area, I jumped from app to app on my phone, sending a few messages to other people who'd offered me help. I was conscious that it was already 3 pm—it was the end of winter, so it would soon be cold and dark.

I waited in the airport for a while, constantly refreshing my phone. I was hopeful but also realistic: it was very last-minute, and it was a huge thing to have a stranger show up for the night with two hours' notice.

I called a few friends while I waited and their energy calmed me, but I would be lying if I said I wasn't starting to worry. Just as I plugged my phone into a charger in the corner, it began to ring in my hand.

It was George, checking to see that I had arrived safely in Melbourne. As soon as he said hello, I noticed another call coming through from an unknown number. I quickly told George I would have to call him back—my accommodation plans had fallen through, and this call could be my solution.

I held my breath as I answered. It was a producer from Triple M, asking if I could do a radio interview while I was in Melbourne. I thanked them but said I needed to keep trying for a place to stay.

Just as I hung up, my phone pinged with a text: a hotel in the Melbourne CBD was confirming a night's stay under my name. I was confused but ever so relieved to get this news.

Now I had to figure out how to get to this new accommodation. The hotel was about twenty kilometres away. By now it was close to 5 pm: having spent the past two hours organising myself, the sun had quietly vanished by the time I walked out of the terminal. I only had about twenty dollars in my pocket, having run into a few unexpected costs for food and transport during my stay on the South Coast. I was tired and it was cold, and as I started the long walk towards the city, which my phone estimated would take about four hours, it began to rain. It was just drizzle at first, but the longer I walked, the heavier it got.

I pulled the hood of my hoodie up as options circled in my head. I was still a long way away from a tram stop, but I could jump in a taxi for twenty dollars' worth of distance to at least get me closer to the hotel—or I could keep walking, risk getting sick from the cold and wet air, but hold on to enough money to pay for a hot meal somewhere.

I stopped underneath a shop awning to take stock, but my decision became an easy one when I noticed a vacant taxi approaching. I stuck my damp arm out and hailed it down.

'Where to?' asked the driver.

'Elizabeth Street, please,' I said. 'Sorry, I'm drenched. I'll take my hoodie off so it doesn't soak your seat.'

'Don't worry about it, love,' the driver said with a smile. 'That seat has seen far worse. You look familiar. Where are you from?'

'I've come from Sydney; I'm on a bit of a journey. It's hard to explain, but being in here sure beats walking in the rain. Oh, I almost forgot to mention—I only have twenty dollars on me, so if you could get me as close to Elizabeth Street as possible, that would be awesome. I'll hop out when the meter hits twenty dollars.'

'Hang on!' he said. His posture straightened up in his seat. 'I know who you are. You're that woman living on the streets! What's your name—Kate?'

'It's Kath, actually—nice to meet you,' I said, surprised.

'I'm Matt.'

'Great to meet you, Matt. Thanks for doing this.'

'I was only talking about you with my sister the other day! We've been following you online for the past few weeks. I can't believe you're in my taxi! Can we get a photo before you go?'

I was flattered—I had only been recognised a handful of times by strangers, all of whom had seen the various media

I'd done and the distinct Kindness Factory hoodie that I wore everywhere as a uniform.

I told Matt about the conversations I'd had with George, and that I'd come to Melbourne trusting my gut that everything would be okay. Taking the journey outside New South Wales felt like a big deal at the time, and at that point I had no idea just how far I would end up going on the journey.

'Kath, are you sure about this?' Matt asked me, concerned. 'What does this man want with you?'

Just like the teachers in Goulburn who had been worried about me accepting a lift with Damo, I could tell that Matt was suspicious. 'I don't know,' I said. 'Honestly. But we're meeting in a public place tomorrow, so I think I'm pretty safe.'

'I don't know how you're doing this, Kath,' he replied, shaking his head. 'There are any number of things that could go wrong.'

I smiled. 'There's also a lot that could go right, though. That's what this whole journey is about. Believing in the kindness of strangers to get me through. I haven't been let down yet, so I'm going to continue to believe everything will be okay.'

'What do you mean?'

'Well, in any moment in life things can go one way or another, right? Sometimes we just have to trust that everything will be okay.'

Matt wasn't convinced, and to be fair to him, I could see why.

'You're leaving a lot to chance in this situation, though, aren't you?' he asked with a grimace.

His words left me a little rattled. But I reminded myself of everything that had happened already—the journey to date had given me no reason to believe that this wasn't a good idea.

Matt shook his head again. 'You're a better person than I am, Kath.'

I didn't consider myself any better than Matt for having the outlook I did, but if I hadn't had a positive approach to most of my life's adversities, I told him, I probably wouldn't be walking, and I certainly wouldn't be in his car.

'I'd love to know more about that. I read that you've broken your back—twice? How on earth *are* you walking?'

'I put it down to a lot of things,' I said, thinking about it as I watched the red taillights of the car in front. 'Most of the time when I was in rehab, I had no idea what I'd be up against each day. But I also knew that the worst thing I could do in those days was nothing. So I tried. Every single day, I'd take two steps more than the previous day, and over time that added up. I knew in those moments that if I put in the effort, eventually everything would be okay.'

Matt smiled. 'I guess you're a glass-half-full kind of person, then?'

I didn't exactly have an answer for that, but I fumbled my way through. 'Maybe. I reckon being positive is not so much about not having difficulties in life, but knowing that we all have difficulties and challenges sometimes. It's alright to find things hard. What always helped me on those hard days was believing there were better days ahead. No one will sail through life without any tough moments. But in those moments, one of the most important things you can do for yourself is believe that it will get better—because more often than not, it will.'

'I really like that. Where'd you learn all of this?' Matt asked, flicking on his indicator.

A lot of the people in my life had shown me the power of positivity, but none more so than my brother Grant. As I described him to Matt, I realised he must be one of the most positive people I'd ever met. He was also one of my best friends, and I just loved spending time with him. Plus, I'd lived through it—I learned to walk again when everyone told me it was close to impossible, so I've come to believe things can always get better. That's one of the beauties of life.

I relaxed back in my seat, not knowing when the fare would run out, while cranking up the heating in the car to warm myself up. Grant and I always shared a special bond. A lot of his person- ality comes from our grandfather in Finley, whom we adore.

I realised then, in my reflection of Grant, that positivity was always something that came pretty naturally to me—sure, I'd had bad days, like anyone does, but they'd always been few and far between. Grant and Pa had both taught me that there are always better times ahead. Having been through the wringer a few times in my life already, I knew without a doubt that this was true.

• • •

Rehab was never something I looked forward to, as an inpatient or outpatient. The place is just not conducive to thriving in any way—from the mental barrier of facing in to your recovery every day to the stale colour of the off-white walls you're surrounded by. I was glad to be free of the grind of appointment after appointment when I felt like I had better things to do.

The reality, though, was that I wasn't all that busy outside of work, and I missed having a goal to strive towards—something cricket had always given me. It had been eighteen months since I'd first entered rehab, but it felt like a lifetime.

Knowing that my recovery from this point would be predominantly based in a pool and on a bike, one of my doctors suggested that I might like to try triathlon—I'd only have to add in a run to cover all three disciplines. I initially laughed at his suggestion, but after thinking on it a little more, I gave my brother Grant a call to see if he might like to join me.

It wasn't long before we both fell in love with the endurance sport. All the time we spent running, riding and swimming helped me clear my head of the worries that would sometimes find me—training had always seemed to put me in a better frame of mind.

The thing I loved most about training with Grant was that he is genuinely one of the most upbeat blokes you could ever meet. I reckon if you crashed into his car, he would get out and just be glad to have the opportunity to meet you. He would genuinely be excited about the weather even if you were swapping insurance details in the rain. People often get the fright of their life when they're walking beside Grant in a public place and he bursts out in to song, then looks at you expecting you to join in as if it's the most normal thing in the world. The more time I spent with him—training but also just being—the more his positivity rubbed off on me.

As much as I loved the training, I wasn't overly fussed about doing triathlons competitively. Living with the disability that I had at that time, without much feeling below my left knee, I'd only just started feeling confident in my physical abilities and I was just happy to have regained enough mobility to be training. So I was shocked when I compared some of my training times to the times of athletes doing ironman events, and I realised that I was probably fitter than I thought. Grant knew this too, and he convinced me that we should sign up for a half-ironman—a 1.8 kilometre swim, 90 kilometre bike ride and a 21.1 kilometre run. We had plenty of time to train and because the event was in Mooloolaba on the Sunshine Coast we figured that we could make it a bit of a family holiday.

I hadn't been so sure initially, and I knew I'd have to up my training a couple of notches to meet the demands of the course. But we got ourselves a proper program and stuck to it. My main goal was to finish, which I felt confident I could do, especially as some of our family were making the trip to the Sunshine Coast to cheer us on.

Grant taught me to love the process of training, rather than the outcome we were hoping for. I reckon I could have forgiven myself for pulling out of any of our winter pool sessions—which we mostly did in the evening in an outdoor unheated pool—but I knew Grant would always be there, singing a song on the pool's edge while jumping up and down to psych himself up.

His positive energy always lifted me, and it was because of him that I was able to cross the finish line in Mooloolaba with a smile on my face—and with a time so good that it earned me a ticket into the full ironman event to be held in six months' time. I was hooked.

This was the first time since my first serious back injury that I felt like myself again. The turnaround was due to a lot of things—a combination of gratitude, friendship and positivity, among other things, but also the passing of time, which can soften the effects of grief. Surrounding myself with positive people was a way to remind myself to be positive, which in turn energised me to adopt more positive behaviours and show kindness towards myself and others.

It's a lot easier to be kind to yourself and others when you have a positive frame of mind. The way I got there was through gratitude—and the two work nicely hand in hand.

• • •

'So you're down to your last twenty dollars?' Matt the taxi driver asked.

I nodded, checking the meter that had been ticking along while we were talking. I was shocked to see it read eighteen dollars and five cents.

'Tell you what, Kath,' said Matt, 'it's been a real treat to meet you in person. What say I do you a deal? If you can get thirty likes on our photo on Facebook in ten minutes, I'll waive the fare and you can buy yourself a meal. Sound like a deal?'

I agreed, knowing this would be an easy win for me. I'm pretty sure Matt knew it too.

Sitting in the front passenger seat, I stuck out my arm and captured a snap of us, then posted the photo. I had ten likes in under a minute—and 30 in just two minutes!

Matt and I got caught in bumper-to-bumper traffic for the next 40 minutes, and chatted the entire time. I learned about his life, his achievements and failures to date, and as we shared more we went from being strangers to friends.

I've got to be honest here: when I first got into his taxi, I was barely up for a hello. I was worried about getting to the hotel, and with my stomach grumbling from hunger, I knew I'd have nothing to eat until the next day.

When we're in those moments of wondering how things will turn around, the most important thing to keep in mind is that they *could*. They won't always, but you need to take comfort in knowing that it's at least possible.

When I reached the hotel, they welcomed me warmly and told me my mini-bar and breakfast had been paid for, and they were going to bring a bottle of champagne to my room.

At that moment my phone pinged again—it was a text message from George, asking if I was okay. As I juggled my bag and damp hoodie, I texted him back to let him know that someone had come through and that I would see him on the weekend. He didn't respond.

Entering that hotel room was a relief. I had a roof over my head, and I could dry my clothes off. Then, as I looked around, I realised that I also had a voucher for some room service. I tucked into a few cookies from the mini bar and then selected some things from the menu, all the while feeling deeply grateful that everything had worked out.

When my meal arrived, there was too much food for me to finish. With appreciation for how very fortunate I was in that moment, I put my hoodie back on and packaged up the uneaten food, plus a few snacks from the mini bar, and ventured back outside, looking for someone who might be doing it tough. Sadly, it didn't take me too long to find a young woman—and she looked far too young to be living on the cold winter streets of Melbourne.

'Hi, I'm Kath,' I said. 'I have a bit of leftover food. I haven't touched it, and most of it's still warm. A bit of fish, some mash and vegies. Have you eaten?'

'I'm Jessie,' she replied. 'Thanks for the offer. I'm not all that hungry, actually, just cold. Don't suppose you have any cash?'

'Jessie, this might sound hard to believe, but I don't have more than twenty dollars. It's a long story, but I'm living night to night myself. What do you need that I can get you with twenty dollars?'

'If I could save that cash, I could put it towards a night in a hostel in the next few days, for a warm shower and to wash some clothes. Would that be okay?'

'You need a shower?'

'I would love a shower.'

'Jessie, I'm staying about a hundred metres from here. Why don't you come with me now—you can have a shower in my room. Let's grab your stuff so it's safe. I'll look after it while you're in the shower.'

Jessie looked at me with wary eyes. I could tell she wasn't sure about this, but the thought of a warm shower was too hard to refuse. She asked me why I was offering her help, and I told her I'd had some good luck that day and I wanted to share it. She half-smiled.

Jessie took a long shower, and came out looking like a completely different person, the harshness of living rough on the streets washed from her skin. She sat down with me and ate the meal I'd offered her earlier, and we got chatting again.

'Thanks for the shower,' she began. 'I needed it.'

'It's no worries. Glad I could give you that, if nothing else. Actually, here's the twenty dollars. Anything else I can do for you?'

'Nothing else, thank you.'

Jessie was silent then, but for some reason I felt the need to keep going.

'How did you end up on the streets—if you don't mind me asking?'

'Bad luck, I guess.'

I looked down, struggling to find words that might offer comfort. I'm sure Jessie sensed this as she kept talking.

'My dad left when I was young. Mum got a boyfriend, and he abused Mum and my two sisters. I started staying at a friend's house, on their couch, and that helped for a while but then she got into drugs and her parents blamed me, even though I was trying to stop her from using. I went to another friend's house, but then the parents of the first friend told those parents what they thought about me, and I had to go back home. Then Mum's boyfriend laid into me, so the streets are the safest place for me at the moment. I have a crew I can sleep next to sometimes, but tonight I was trying to get closer to the city to see if I could get some cash for a wash.'

I swallowed the lump in my throat, wanting to say something, but nothing came out.

'I'm not sure if I believe your reasons for helping me,' Jessie continued. 'It feels like there's something else going on. I don't really care, but I think I'll leave in a minute if that's okay with you . . .'

The last thing I wanted in this moment was to be condescending—or, worst of all, to make her feel unsafe. But it was important to me that she knew my intentions were good and I was coming from a sincere place. I felt that sharing some more of myself, my background and what I was doing might help. Her eyes grew bigger the more I went on, but she stayed quiet and listened intently.

Jessie was engaged in the conversation, but I wasn't sure how she was feeling—the expression on her face remained blank. I felt like a complete fraud. There I was telling a young homeless person that I had left the safety of my home and support networks to do some kind of social experiment, which I could back out of whenever I chose. As I tried to explain, I felt like I was blabbering.

'Are you religious?' Jessie asked.

'No, I'm not.'

'So, what have you learned so far?' she asked.

I thought for a few moments. 'So far, I haven't wanted or needed anything. People have shown up for me. I've been fed well, I've always had a roof over my head and a bed to sleep in. And I've met some pretty phenomenal people. You're one of them.'

'Me?' she asked.

'Absolutely!'

'There's nothing so great about me.'

But there was everything so great about Jessie. Despite everything she had been through, and was still going through, she was still here and fighting to make a better life for herself. I didn't know much about her, but I understood that she had to be strong. To have survived as long as she had when a lot of people had done wrong by her was admirable, to say the very least. And to continue to keep going when a lot of others might have given up.

I really wanted to help her. 'Jessie, if you could ask for one thing from someone, what would it be?' I asked.

'I need a job.'

'How old are you?' I asked.

'I'm eighteen.'

'Any skills?'

'I can clean . . .'

'Let me make a few calls. Can you wait here a while with me?'

I grabbed my phone and called a few Melbourne friends. I told them I'd met someone who was a little down on their luck and who needed a job, and asked if they knew anyone who needed a cleaner. I was certain that we would reach someone eventually. And within five minutes we did.

'Our building needs a cleaner,' one friend said. 'Who do you have in mind? What's their company? I'll check it all out and come back to you tomorrow.'

I didn't want the person on the other end of the phone thinking that this was some way-out notion, or worrying that because Jessie didn't have a company behind her she would be unreliable. I knew deep down—call it a gut feeling—that Jessie would show up and clean that building as it had never been cleaned before. She was simply looking for an opportunity.

'Can she meet me at ten am tomorrow?' my friend asked.

'Leave it with me. Text me the address, and expect to see Jessie tomorrow at ten am.'

I hung up and looked over at Jessie, who was watching me with wide eyes. At first she wasn't sure what was going on, but I could see hope in her eyes as she started to well up. She told me that no one had ever done anything like that for her before.

I just wanted to get up and hug the life back into her, and tell her that I was sure everything would be okay. But I knew that wasn't realistic. This job prospect was just a tiny sliver of hope—a lot of other things had to go right for something concrete to come of it. *But why*, I wondered, *has no one ever helped this person before?*

• • •

All in all, my day had been a good one. There were a few stressful moments, but by the end of it, not only did I have a roof over my head and a warm bed to sleep in, but Jessie might have a chance at a new beginning the next day.

This wasn't all down to positivity, of course. It took a lot of collaboration—and some might even say luck—that this person was taking a chance on a new cleaner. What I can say I have learned about positivity is this: it isn't defined by the absence of struggle or worry, or even by negative emotions. Sometimes, positivity can simply be the hope that, one day, things will get better.

Living in the world that we do, with social media high-light reels so prominent, it's easy to compare our everyday lives with the best moments other people have had. No one will go through their life without adversity or hardship. Our circumstances can change, but ultimately we choose how we respond. One thing I know is that maintaining hope and belief amid all of my challenges has made them so much more bearable, even when I've been in the trenches fighting to get out.

Jessie and I agreed to meet at the hotel room again the next day at 7 am, and she showered and put on the only clean set of clothes she had. Jessie got the job, cleaning an office block one day per week, which gave her enough income over a couple of weeks to buy some more clothes. A month later, after a solid endorsement, she cleaned the building next door on another day a week, and soon enough she was able to afford a room at a hostel, which ensured her safety.

I'm not sure what she's up to these days, as we lost touch not long after she started her own cleaning business with a friend she'd met on the streets. But wherever she is and whatever she's doing, I hope that Jessie is safe, with a roof over her head and food in her belly each night.

Collaboration

My journey to date had been incredible but also exhausting. I was now in another state, Victoria, further from the safety and comfort of my apartment in Mortdale—which already felt a lifetime away. After my experience with Jessie, it's safe to say that I was on a bit of a high. What started out as a journey of self-discovery and me feeling lost had already led to me being able to help another person in a tangible way, and I felt quite proud of that.

I was excited to meet Beth, who was the very proud owner of a coffee shop in Heidelberg Heights. She had offered to put me up for the night and even teach me how to make a coffee. Beth and her partner Hatty lived close to the cafe, but they drove to South Melbourne to pick me up, and then shouted me dinner at one of their favourite restaurants. They had an early start at the cafe the next day, so when we got back to their place they told me to get a good night's rest and find my way to the cafe when I woke up.

By this point of the trip, as much as I was learning and enjoying myself, I had started to get a little weary and a sleep-in was really appealing to me. But as I drifted off to sleep, I decided that I really wanted the whole cafe experience with Beth. I set my alarm for 5.30 am to make sure I was showered and ready to get stuck in.

It was a small cafe, but the only one for three blocks. They opened at 6 am, and Beth explained to me that they had regular customers who would be counting on them to have everything set up in time to make their orders of coffee and breakfast for the commute into the city for work. As a kid in high school, I had worked in a sandwich shop on a Thursday night for a little bit of pocket money, so I hoped naively that I would be useful. But with Beth on the coffee machine pumping out coffees and Hatty looking after the food and front of house, the place ran like absolute clockwork. They were a great team and you could tell that they had worked together for a long time. I felt like I was getting in the way, so I took myself out the back and started washing some of the dishes that had started to pile up. It didn't feel like much but as the pile started to disappear in front of me, I noticed another pile not too far away that had started to stack up, so I grabbed them too—it was nice to be contributing in a way that felt helpful. As I cleared the second and third pile, Beth appeared. It was 8 am now—the time had been flying by—and the wave of customers had started to ease.

She coaxed me out towards the coffee machine, which smelled delicious. I love coffee and had always wanted to learn how to make one from a proper machine, which I think Beth realised from the many questions I asked the night before. So she started showing me how best to froth the milk, and at what level depending on the type of coffee. I was fascinated by how much effort went in to making what I had always assumed to be a simple drink that I had ordered on the daily for most of my adult life.

Despite her thoughtful instruction, I was initially pretty terrible at making them, so when I saw a customer approach the counter close to the coffee machine, I took a backward step. Beth explained to the customer that I was in training, and told her a little bit about the journey I was on. The customer became adamant that I make her coffee. She was in no hurry, and if I buggered it up too much, we could start again.

• • •

As I slipped back into the rhythm of full-time work, more and more people learned about my story and I was asked questions—mostly well-intentioned—about my life. Some were baffled that I was as carefree and comfortable as I appeared to be. In truth, I was struggling, and the people closest to me knew it, but to strangers it wasn't obvious.

I still felt so lost. Why had I gone through all these big life experiences? And what did they mean? Yes, I had a great job, and thanks to my sense of humour I was able to laugh and smile through most days. (Upon reflection, though, I see that was probably a defence mechanism, helping me hide from my feelings.) But if I couldn't answer these 'how and why' questions in my own mind, then how on earth would I be able to explain them to others? I started searching a little deeper within myself for the answers.

I'd been through a lot, but I knew I couldn't take full credit for my ability to smile in the office every day. A lot of support and kindness had helped me. The people around me while I was in the depths of my trauma had got me through moments I wouldn't have survived on my own. I thought back to the kindness of Bobby, the security guard who had helped me when my leg was due to be amputated, or of the stranger who could see that I couldn't reach the lift button from my wheelchair. Kindness is powerful, and it was the thing connecting the hardest days of my life with my current disposition—kindness was the thing that had saved me.

When I realised this one Saturday morning, I was energised like I had never been before. I had been so lucky to have received as much kindness as I had, and now that I was well enough, physically and mentally, to be the giver of kindness, I was going to do exactly that. In that moment, as I sat in my kitchen eating fruit salad, the Kindness Factory was born.

It started as a social media page to record acts of goodness. I knew how to navigate my way around Facebook and Instagram, so that seemed the best way to get the idea out there. And what was the idea, exactly? Simple: to spread as much kindness as possible, knowing that small acts of kindness can create big change.

After designing a page that invited people to share acts of kindness, I made it live and started to invite some of my friends to follow along. That prompted a flow of questions. 'What is it?' they would ask.

'I'm going to post acts of kindness on here,' I would reply. 'Hopefully we get a groundswell of people to do the same.'

And sure enough, as the days and weeks went by, it started to catch on.

I started small. On the way to work one morning, the orange petrol light blinked on in my car. As I drove into the petrol station, I decided that I would pay for the tank of the first person I saw. Simple. The only problem was, there was no one else there. I hung around awkwardly by the bowsers after I'd finished fuelling up, until the cashier started to glare at me through the station's window.

I conceded defeat, but promised myself that I would call in at the same petrol station on my way home and go through with it then. Even so, I was a bit disappointed that the idea hadn't worked out as perfectly as I had scripted it in my head.

As I started walking towards the register to pay for my fuel, I spotted a black and white mini driving over the speed bump and pulling up at the bowser next to my car. This was it! My opportunity to offer kindness to someone else.

I'd felt so clear in my mind about what I would say and how I would say it, but as I approached the driver, the words I'd been practising in my head started to get all jumbled.

The lady's smile was wide as I approached—and she didn't even know what I was about to do.

'Hi,' I began nervously. 'I'm Kath . . . I, er, I'd love to shout you your tank of fuel today if that's okay.'

'Sure!' she replied, then she began to digest what I had just said. 'Hang on—what do you mean? You want to pay for my petrol?'

'Yeah, that's it. No strings attached. I simply want to pay for your petrol. That's it.'

'I'm a little confused. I mean, of course you can pay for my petrol, but why do you want to?' the woman asked.

'No real reason,' I lied. And then I reconsidered. If I wanted her to accept my offer in the spirit I was making it, I needed to explain a little more about my intentions. 'Look, I've been through a fair bit in life over the last few years, but I'm doing okay now,' I started. 'I recently realised that I have been lucky enough to receive a lot of kindness and goodwill from many people, and I've decided that I want to give back.'

As we walked towards the register together and I explained a little more of my life to date, the woman—whose name was Lucy—almost begged to pay for my petrol instead. But eventually she agreed that she would let me do this. We chatted for about twenty minutes or so and I learned a lot about her too. She became the very first act of kindness in the movement that is the Kindness Factory.

What I could never have known at that moment was that Lucy would show up on my kindness journey years later and shout me dinner on that first night. It was a nice moment for us both—both to see how far the Kindness Factory had come, but also to understand the growth we'd both experienced as people.

• • •

Lucy shared the story of me shouting her petrol on social media later that night. It seemed to attract a fair bit of attention online, which made me uncomfortable. I wasn't doing this for notoriety or recognition, and I was a little embarrassed when people started sharing the post. Then I realised that a lot of people had been inspired, and similar acts started to roll into my newsfeed.

Kindness, I found, was contagious. When kindness is shared, it can inspire more kindness. And sometimes we need to work together to allow the magic to happen.

I still had no idea what the Kindness Factory was, or what it would or could be, but as I started to receive more questions, from both strangers and friends, a narrative started to form. Friends brainstormed with me about campaigning, others helped me design logos on the back of napkins at the local pub, and still others kept the acts of kindness coming in over social media. Before I knew it, someone reached out with an offer to design a website to house all these stories of human connection.

I get a lot of credit for starting the Kindness Factory—and, don't get me wrong, I am proud to have done so—but it wouldn't be what it is without all these people coming together to make it happen. Collaboration was the key to its foundation, and it continues to be today as we work at building a kinder world. We have a great board of directors, for example, who each have their own skill set that adds value and diversity of experience to ensure that we have gold standard governance, and that we are making decisions to serve the community in accordance with the Kindness Factory's mission and values. The most beautiful thing is that anyone who has become involved is there for the right reasons. We have all been connected by our common purpose.

In the early days, I made a point of not getting lost in what this idea could grow into—I stayed true to its small beginnings, and focused on doing practical things like shouting dinners for the homeless. I wanted not just to provide people with a meal but to sit with them and enjoy the experience of eating together.

Next I raised money for kids who needed wheelchairs, and shouted a stranger a coffee each day on my way to work. Simple gestures, as I knew very well, could completely change someone's day. Sometimes the smallest thing—like holding a door open for someone, or looking them in the eye and saying g'day, or even just smiling at a stranger as they walked past— could have an immediate impact. No act of kindness is a waste of effort.

For a while, small opportunities presented themselves almost daily. The Kindness Factory's social media pages had taken off, and we were now followed by thousands of people. I was hearing from strangers all over the world who were inspired to do more in celebration of kindness. Among all the messages that I was receiving, though, there was one that stood out to me; the subject line was simply 'Checking in'.

The email was from a man to whom I felt I owed a great deal. Mark was a volunteer with an organisation called Limbs

4 Life, who had been incredibly decent to me in the days before I was due to have my leg amputated. The organisation had helped me understand what to expect, and how to cope with the life-altering surgery. Mark, an amputee himself, had volunteered to help with the plans to make my home more disability-friendly in the leadup to what would have been my amputation, and to be available if I needed someone to talk to. I thought of him often, and I felt such gratitude for his organisation, but I hadn't reached out to let them know what their support had meant to me.

I wrote back to Mark as soon as I could, letting him know how I was, and arranged to catch up with him to say thanks in person. When we met up, Mark put me in touch with the CEO of Limbs 4 Life, Mel Noonan, and before long I met up with her too, and she told me her story.

One day Mel was running late for a meeting. She was rushing to jump on a train, but misjudged and found herself stuck between the train and the platform as the train moved off. She was lucky to have survived. She spent three months in a coma, and then woke up to the news that she had lost both her legs in the accident. Only after a very lengthy period of rehabilitation was she able to get back to her regular life.

At the time, Mel had never met anyone who had lost a limb before, and she found the experience incredibly daunting. So when she was well enough to do so, she created Limbs 4 Life, a peer-to-peer service which connected those who had lost limbs and were now living well with those who were about to face that challenge, or who were struggling with the transition.

As we sat in a coffee shop chatting, I realised pretty quickly that Mel was someone I admired greatly. She was the type of woman who never complained, who got on with her day the best way that she knew how to, and who always looked out for others and wanted to help. Those qualities resonated with me.

I had wondered a lot what my life would have looked like if my leg had been amputated. I liked to think that I would have responded the way Mel had, but if I had to guess, I don't think I would have done it with anything like the grace and dignity she had.

After we had chatted for a while, I felt I could ask her what I considered a pretty personal question: 'Mel, what do you miss most about having two normal, healthy legs?'

She smiled, and told me her response would make me laugh.

I waited expectantly.

'Burpees,' said Mel. 'I really miss being able to do burpees!'

I did laugh. Not because she couldn't do burpees, but because I couldn't think of anyone on the planet who would miss such a thing. When I was an athlete, they were often handed out as punishment; for me they were the part of training I dreaded the most.

By the end of our conversation, I'd had an idea. I wanted to combine this quirk of Mel's with my desire to give back to the organisation that had given me so much. I made a deal with her there and then. Now that I had physically recovered from my injuries, I would complete one burpee for every one dollar donated to Limbs 4 Life. I thought that was an achievable goal: I didn't know too many people, after all. I expected I might raise $100 if I did well.

That night, I shared the story online and started a GoFundMe page. I shared the link with a few friends, and when I checked the account an hour later I nearly fell over. We'd already raised $3000! That was a lot of burpees . . . I was going to have to start training.

As more and more people shared the link and the total kept rising, I realised I was going to need some help. As far as I'd come in my physical recovery, thousands of burpees was not something I could do on my own. I started recruiting friends and family who I knew I could count on to help me bring this dream to life.

As the story spread more widely, I was shocked to see more and more money flow into the account. It was great to see, but it was also very daunting as the tally of burpees was growing with every dollar. By the end of that week, and after a segment on Channel 7 News, I'd begun to doubt that we could do them all—over 20,000 burpees!

Logistically, it was going to be a nightmare to count all the burpees, so a few of us came up with the idea to use tokens that represented ten burpees—there'd be 2000 in all. We'd gather at the local fire station close to Mum and Dad's place in Mortdale to undertake the challenge. For every ten burpees someone did, they'd take a token and put it in a bucket. When there were no tokens left, the burpees would be complete.

Now, ten burpees might not sound like a lot, but when you're doing them with not much rest in between, they soon start to wear you down. There were people at that hall doing burpees who I'd known for years, from my three-year-old nephews to my 85-year-old grandma. It was incredible to see people from all walks of life and from diverse backgrounds come together to attempt this unusual goal.

As odd as completing that many burpees sounds, it is no mean feat! The room was chaotic, and yet there was never a doubt in anyone's mind that we would get those burpees done. There was high-fiving, clapping and cheering, and zero ego. Three hundred people had contributed.

At the end of the challenge, I stood up to say a few words of thanks. I hadn't noticed until then how many strangers there were in the room. In fact, I reckon I only knew about 100 of those who had gathered. Sometimes people just need an offer to get involved in helping do good. It's amazing to think about what we can achieve when we work together.

There is no way we would have punched out that many burpees with just a few people doing them. Collaborating with nearly 300 other people had brought out the best in every person in that room, as we cheered each other to go further, harder and longer. We were all exhausted at certain points, but not one of us gave up, not wanting to let the rest of the team down. We each had each other's backs and worked together to get the job done.

It was a pretty phenomenal feeling. There's a lot to be said for sharing a common purpose with others, as it tends to bring out the best in us. What had brought us together on this day was the desire to help others—a wish to offer kindness. Our goal had real meaning, and collaboration is so much more achievable when you have purpose like that. The whole experience only spurred me to grow the Kindness Factory even more.

The day was honestly one of the best of my life. To be able to give back to an organisation that had given me so much in such an uncertain period of my life meant the world to me— but seeing the joy on Mel's face as we powered through those burpees together was also pretty special.

● ● ●

It took me three goes to get that first customer's latte to at least look like it was consumable. As the morning rolled on, both Beth and Hatty encouraged me relentlessly, guiding me to a better pour of coffee each time. The customers even occasionally chimed in with encouraging words, which helped me to relax. Making cafe-quality coffee is hard, I learned. But like anything, if you want to be better at it, you just have to keep practising. And the task becomes so much more manageable, and even enjoyable, when you have people supporting you and helping you get to the end goal. The same goes for any job, task or process in life. Thankfully for me, Beth and Hatty were both in need of their morning caffeine hit too, and brave enough to entrust me with the task.

'Cappuccino for me please; extra hot,' said Hatty.

Beth called over, 'I'll have a flat white, thanks boss—extra shot of coffee for me.'

Hatty had cooked the two of them a small bite to eat and it felt really good to be able to look after the place, serving them a coffee and watching them put their feet up for a meal, even if it was only for ten minutes before the next wave of customers came through. It took a team to make the engine of this small but busy cafe work. Be it a sporting team, family, school classroom or even corporate environment, whenever there is more than one of us and there is a shared goal in mind, more often than not, we are a team. Different personalities can sometimes complicate the dynamic, but ego has no place in collaboration. Everyone has different strengths and weaknesses; accepting that means you're more likely to look for another person's complementary strengths when you're collaborating. It takes patience and communication to collaborate well; and it is never really perfect. In that tiny Melbourne cafe, feeling useful and purposeful as part of the coffee team, reminded me of one of the best parts of kindness—not only does practising kindness help others, it also makes you feel really bloody good.

Empathy

One o'clock, Centre Place. My shout, see you then.

That was the text I had received from George, the man who had flown me to Melbourne from Sydney. I knew nothing more than his first name, and that so far he had been incredibly generous to me. I had a sneaking suspicion that he was the one who had put me up for the night at the hotel.

The day after my barista lesson with Beth and Hatty, I met some Cricket Australia staff at the Melbourne Cricket Ground (MCG) for a late breakfast. It was close to a three-kilometre walk from the MCG to Centre Place, where I was meeting George. Even if I had cash, that was walkable, and the weather was better today. My stomach twisted and turned as I neared Centre Place, and all the questions people had been putting to me flooded my mind. What was I doing? I had no idea what

George wanted from me. Why had he flown me all that way to Melbourne—to meet at a coffee shop, of all places?

The walk didn't take me long, so I had some time to kill. On my journey so far, I had enjoyed having the odd moment to myself, when I could enjoy the experience without having to explain my story to anyone. But in this moment, being alone allowed my mind to go into overdrive, and I couldn't calm my thoughts.

I rang Whip to chat it out with her. 'Mate, I'm waiting right now to meet a bloke named George. He's the one who flew me here.'

'What for?'

'I actually don't know. Which is why I'm calling. He's asked me to meet him in a cafe in Melbourne, in Centre Place. You know it?'

'Oh yeah, sure I do. What's on there?'

'I don't know! I think either lunch or a coffee. I have no money, so I already feel rude about that. I'll just have to wait and see.'

'You sound worried . . . Is everything okay?'

'I guess I'm not really worried, maybe just a little vague on the details. It probably would have helped if I'd asked a few more questions, but I'm here now and he's not too far away. Actually, wow, I didn't realise the time—I should probably get going.'

'Take care, mate. Stay safe. Give me a ring when you finish up so I know that it all went okay.'

'Thanks, Whip. Will do.'

I hung up the phone. My hands were sweaty, and it was 12.55 pm. I stood beside a safety bollard, resting my left leg against it without thinking. When I realised, I lost my balance and nearly fell over. It had been nearly eight months since my bike accident, and my leg had been causing me problems with balance ever since.

• • •

'No, no, no!'

'You're okay, Kath, you're okay,' said Erin.

'Kath, can you hear me?' asked an unfamiliar voice. 'Stay awake if you can. We're calling an ambulance now—the hospital isn't far away. Stay awake if you can.'

When I jolted into consciousnesses, I was lying on my right side, almost face-down on the road, my nose so close to the bitumen that I could smell it softening in the sun. I had my bike helmet on and my sunglasses were pushing into my face. An off-duty firefighter named Mike had stopped his car to assist as we waited for the ambulance.

While on a training ride, I had just been hit by a four-wheel drive.

'Ambulance, please. My best friend has just been hit by a car.' I could hear the panic in Erin's voice as she passed on more information to the ambulance. 'I think it was doing about sixty kilometres per hour. Yes, she was wearing a helmet. I'm not sure if her head has been injured.'

Now Erin turned to me. 'Kath, they'll be here any minute. Where does it hurt the most?'

'My back is killing me,' I managed to say. 'I can't feel my legs. It's all gone. Are my legs okay?'

'Let's try to get this helmet off you so you can breathe a little easier. How's that sound?'

As big and masculine as Mike looked, he took great care as he removed my helmet—and he was right, it did make breathing easier.

'How are your sunnies feeling, Kath? Want me to leave them on, or can I take them off for you?'

I could barely string any words together. I wanted my glasses off—they felt like they were cutting into my face—but I had lost my words. Thankfully, Mike seemed to understand what I wanted and took them off for me. He must have sensed my urgency for pain relief as well, and began answering the question that was in my mind: *Where on earth is the ambulance?*

'Let me check,' he said, and I saw him gesturing towards Erin, who was still on the call. 'It's about five minutes away. Not long now, matey. Just try and stay awake for us, okay?'

Those five minutes felt like an eternity as I lay there holding Erin's hand, her gentle and reassuring squeezes every so often making the pain slightly more bearable.

When I was in the ambulance, I went in and out of consciousness. The pain had started to ease thanks to the relief that the paramedics had put into my right arm. I was in a neck brace and flat on my back, with full lights and sirens taking me to the closest spinal trauma unit, at Royal North Shore Hospital. It wasn't a long drive, but every bump we went over made my back feel like it was breaking.

My arms had started to sting, and I noticed that the sheets dangling off my stretcher were red with blood. The most confronting thing was that I was so injured I had no idea where it was actually coming from. My back and hip hurt the most, while my arms were stinging from what I was guessing was a lot of gravel rash. I continued the mental body scan that I had begun, and I closed my eyes. My right wrist was aching, and my neck was aching. My legs . . . I still couldn't feel one of my legs.

'Kath, stay awake for us, okay,' said the paramedic. 'What were you doing out there on your bike this morning? Where were you off to?'

I remember being really annoyed at her for asking that. Was she serious? I'd just been hit by a car, and my body felt like it was falling apart. I know now that she was just doing her job, trying to distract me and keep me awake, as no doubt I was showing concussion symptoms as well.

'Where were you off to, Kath? Can you answer me?'

'I was off on a ride with my best mate,' I managed to say in response. 'We left this morning. I was going to Manly to have breakfast and a coffee. I'm training for an ironman. Do you think I'll still be able to race? It's in May.'

'Let's just get you to the hospital and we'll see. How is your pain going? We aren't too far away now. We can give you something stronger once we're inside.'

Because of the nature of my injuries, and what had happened—cyclist versus car at 60 kilometres per hour—I was immediately taken into the intensive-care unit and assessed by a large team. My consciousness wavered through the next few hours of tests and observations with heavy pain medication making it hard to stay awake.

Erin was brilliant. I found out later that she was busy calling my family and loved ones to inform them of the accident, and filling out the medical paperwork and insurance details for me while I underwent the necessary tests. There were no immediately obvious internal injuries, which was great news, but the doctors needed as much information as possible about my medical history so they could be as thorough as possible.

Erin told them I'd had hand surgery, and a number of operations on my back. Hearing this, one of the trauma nurses interrupted. 'What was that surgery called?'

'I had a few laminectomies and something else like that, I think,' I mumbled. 'But the big one was total disc replacement at L5/S1.'

'I'm sorry, did I just hear correctly?' The nurse sounded a little confused. 'You have already broken your back?'

Erin took over. 'Yes, playing cricket a few years ago now. But she's done pretty well to overcome that.'

'I'm going to call in the neuro specialists, girls—I'll be back.'

Erin continued to take down my very long medical history. Meanwhile, the trauma nurse had started assembling a large team of not only specialists, but medical students. As they entered the room and asked for permission to observe, the calmness I had felt in Erin's company started to vanish, and I felt overwhelmed. My unusual medical history seemed to be attracting a big audience. Erin sensed this and asked them to leave, but the specialist stayed back to discuss everything and do another assessment.

'Kath, I'm going to roll you on your side. I know it's painful, but I'd like to do a manual examination. Because of your prior injuries, some of the scans we've ordered will be a little hard to read. I see here that you've had a total disc replacement—is that right?'

The pain had started to find me again, and I could only answer in single words. 'Yes.'

'Unfortunately, the titanium in that prosthetic won't show up on an MRI, so we're going to have to get a little creative, okay?'

I nodded.

'Just try to stay as still as possible for me, Kath. I'll get some help to get you on your side, and then I'll need you to let me know where on your spine hurts the most as I run my fingers down. Does that sound alright?'

'Yes.'

I could sense the seriousness in the specialist's voice.

'Okay—let's roll on one, two, three!' They rolled me onto my side. 'I'm going to start up at your neck, okay? And as I move down, I want you to tell me when it starts to hurt more than just the touch.'

The doctor moved his hands just below my hairline. 'Anything here?'

'No.'

'I'll keep going—you just let me know.'

'Right there,' I said through gritted teeth as the doctor moved down towards the middle area of my spine.

'Okay, take a note of that, please,' the doctor said to one of the nurses. 'Now, I know this hurts, but I'm going to keep running my fingers down and I want you to let me know when the pain starts to ease.'

I couldn't sense how long his finger moved down my spine, but it must have been a pretty significant amount. Imaging later revealing that I had fractures in four separate areas of my spine—at the T12, L1, S3 and S5 vertebrae. My neck wasn't broken, but I would forever have weakness in that area due to the subluxation—an injury not dissimilar to a dislocation. These days it's nearly impossible for me to live without anti-inflammatory medication close by.

I had scan after scan that day, and lay in the emergency ward going in and out of a drug-induced sleep. Erin was there the whole time, holding my hand, and still dressed in the lycra she was wearing during our ride that morning. She spent almost the whole day tending to my needs and keeping everyone updated as best she could. She went home that night for a shower and a brief rest, and was back at 7 am to sit with me again. I was so thankful to have her by my side as we faced this terrible uncertainty.

• • •

My recovery journey after being hit by a car had some similarities with my kindness journey. There were twists and turns,

I had to face the uncertainty of what lay ahead each day, and I needed a little bit of faith every day that I'd get through it.

The reality of what I was facing after the accident was tough. Breaking your back twice is something most people haven't experienced—heck, even breaking it once is pretty rare. So I understand why a lot of people seem to think I have superhuman powers and can bounce back from anything. But I can't. I'm as human as anyone else—I've just had to face challenges that most haven't. Probably that's given people a warped sense of my abilities as a person.

As news of my accident spread, I was inundated by messages from people sorry to hear of my situation and who wanted to wish me well. Many asked what my future looked like. I never felt comfortable answering that, because as the days went on, my prognosis kept getting worse.

My body was a mess. Walking was impossible. Not just because I couldn't use my legs at that point, but because almost all of the walking aids require you to lean on your wrists, and one of mine was broken.

When I look back at that time, it's clear to me that the day after my accident was the toughest. It was one of the most physically painful days, but as the scans of my body continued, the doctors kept finding more breaks and fractures. While the pain made more sense, I knew that my chances of making a full recovery and walking again were low.

Emotionally, I felt ruined. It had taken me so long to get my life back on track after my first round of rehab—in fact, it was only a few months before this accident that I'd begun to feel like myself again. I was exhausted, and now I had to start all over again. I didn't know if I had it in me.

Erin is a very practical person. She prides herself on having a solution-focused mindset, and she doesn't like to sit in any problem without coming up with a plan. That doesn't mean there's always an answer, but if you are Erin, you always try.

The thing I love most about Erin is her no-nonsense attitude—and she is without a doubt the most consistent person I have ever known. You always know where you stand with her. There is never any guessing. She is true to herself always, and regardless of the company she is in, she will always be authentically that way. I see something of her in myself sometimes. I too don't like to sit in the discomfort of uncertainty for too long.

What all this meant was that day one was a huge challenge for both of us.

My mood was altered by the painkillers running through my veins, and I kept drifting in and out of sleep. In the moments my eyes were open, Erin made small talk, but I could sense her brain ticking over as she considered how to fix the situation.

It was midafternoon when I had started to lose a little hope. That was when we learned of the fourth fracture in my spine. While it was a relief to find the fracture, as it explained some of my symptoms, it felt like the hits just kept coming, and I started to crack. The emotion of the past 24 hours hit me hard.

By this point, a physio had been in for an assessment—which felt a little silly because I was a long way from even getting out of bed. She was there to introduce herself, and she encouraged me to elevate the bed so I didn't feel stuck in the one position. Once she left, it was just Erin and me again, and the silence started to make both of us uncomfortable.

I stared blankly at the wall, barely responding to Erin's attempts at conversation. She grabbed my hand and held it tight, and as I looked over at her, I saw tears running down her cheeks—which gave me permission to do the same. We didn't speak, and I think the only time Erin let go of my hand over the next hour was to grab a fresh box of tissues. She gave me the space and safety to feel what I was feeling in that moment. She did so because she felt it too. I knew she was shattered for me, and she was suffering too. In that moment, I knew that my pain was shared. That's what empathy has the power to do.

For me, seeing Erin upset actually hurt more than my injuries. She had always been by my side, through the ups and downs of life, and I owed her the world. And as exhausted as I was at the thought of having to endure all this, it suddenly dawned on me how exhausted she too must have been as she supported me over all these years. Just like she had done before, Erin made me feel like I was the lucky one, as it is much harder to watch someone you care about go through painful experiences. I couldn't imagine how painful it must have been to watch on as I struggled and not be able to do anything about it.

I squeezed Erin's hand back tight, letting her know that everything would be okay. Tomorrow we would start again. *If I walk again*, I told myself, *it will be because of Erin.*

• • •

George was a proper gentleman, opening the cafe door for me and then pulling out my seat for me before he sat. I guessed he was in his early sixties. Well-groomed and nicely dressed, he reminded me a lot of my grandfather from Finley, who believed that presenting yourself well was a way of showing respect and good manners.

'How did you get here today, Kath?' George asked.

'I just walked—I've come from the MCG after a breakfast.'

'How are you managing with money? Do you have a place to stay tonight?'

'I'm short on cash, but not on offers to help. I have the next few nights sorted here in Melbourne, and might be flying to Adelaide in a couple of days' time. So I'm going pretty well, thanks, George. So far so good.'

'What do your parents think of all of this?'

'Should we order something before we get too far into a conversation?' I asked. 'What are you having?' I had noticed a waitress and didn't want her interrupting our conversation any more than she would have to, as already I sensed that this would be an important conversation. After my time in the cafe, I also appreciated hospitality staff more than ever.

'Nothing for me, thanks,' he replied. 'I just came to meet you. Are you hungry? Have you eaten?'

It seemed a little odd that he wasn't ordering anything— it had been his suggestion to meet here, after all. My curiosity about him continued to grow.

'I'm actually okay for food, but I feel like we should order something out of courtesy,' I said. 'Would you mind if I ordered a small coffee?' I didn't have any cash on me, and felt embarrassed that he would have to pay for me even though he wasn't having anything.

'Whatever you like, Kath,' he said. 'My treat.'

The cafe wasn't overly busy, and it wasn't long before the waitress was back with my coffee and some water for the table. George seemed restless. I could sense that he was trying to figure out what to say, and his hands shook ever so slightly as he poured a glass of water for each of us.

'I find your life story fascinating, Kath,' he said eventually.

I've never been comfortable accepting compliments, and I wasn't even sure if what George had just said was a compliment, but I felt my thoughts speeding up and my cheeks starting to redden. But before I could respond, he continued.

'I was telling my daughter about you this morning. She's a little older than you—a mum now, which is wonderful. I haven't seen her for nearly a decade.'

I so badly wanted to ask why, but it didn't feel right, so I just gave a small smile and waited for him to keep going. As the silence built, I could see tears forming in his eyes, and I knew that whatever he said next, it would be important for me to behave as Erin had beside me in that hospital bed. To hold the moment, whatever it was, even if it made me uncomfortable.

George's hands were on top of the table, and he was wringing them together in discomfort. I knew something big was going on for George, and I wanted to offer him uncon-ditional support, so I placed my right hand on top of his, gently squeezing them and he looked into my eyes for the first time.

'I lost my wife about ten years ago to cancer,' George said, then he paused, tears now trickling down his handsome face. 'That's the first time I have ever said that out loud.'

'George, I'm so sorry.'

'I haven't seen my kids in eight years. Two of them are parents now. I haven't met my grandchildren yet. I've been so consumed in missing my wife that I lost touch with my kids. The conversation I had with my daughter this morning was the first one in six years. They must hate me.'

I couldn't speak for George's children, and I had no idea what his family had gone through, but I found it hard to believe that anyone could hate this man. I fumbled to take a napkin from another table and offered it to George as a tissue.

I saw something of myself in him. I had never been great at expressing my emotions, and the busyness of life had always got in the way of me processing the trauma and grief I'd been through. I was glad that, whatever was going on for George in that moment, he was sharing it with someone.

And the more he explained to me, the more I felt for him. Having lost people in my life, I knew that grief wasn't linear, and it followed no timeline. I also knew it affects people in many different ways. But there was one thing I was sure of, after meeting George and hearing what he had to say: regardless of the situation, he would have tried to be the best he could be for his daughters.

George had distanced himself from his children because he didn't want them to see his pain. He feared that it would make their grief and loss all that much harder. Instead, he had thrown himself into his work to distract himself from the anguish he felt in his heart.

That resonated with me, as I had done the same thing in the past, but with exercise. I flogged myself in the gym, so that I'd feel the physical pain of tired muscles rather than the emotional pain of grief and trauma. Tears and therapeutic talk would probably have been much healthier for me, in the long run.

George and I made a pact. We had each other's number. If we ever needed a non-judgemental ear, we would call one another. We understood each other's pain without having to explain it, which meant we could share in it without difficulty. George promised me he would reconnect with his daughters and meet his grandchildren. I promised him that I would stay safe, and that I'd eventually find purpose and happiness again. The irony was that in sharing that twenty-minute coffee with George, I had just found it.

Through my journey, as I began to understand myself a little more, I was learning that empathy was crucial if I was to offer kindness to others. And, thankfully for me, I had never found it hard to find empathy. I think it's the starting place to understand ourselves and others at a deeper level, regardless of where we've come from. When we have empathy for another's experiences and situation, we can act with more kindness towards ourselves and others.

I think this was apparent to both George and me in that cafe in central Melbourne. He had empathy for me, and I had it for him. And we both walked away feeling better about ourselves and each other.

Trust

I had been blogging daily on the old Kindness Factory website for most of my trip and was amazed at how many people had been keeping track of everything that I was getting up to. Lots of Melbourne locals were reading the blog, and hundreds reached out to offer more help while I was there. With each of these offers I was able to meet even more incredible people who offered me fresh perspective, a roof over my head and help getting from place to place.

I said goodbye to Melbourne and headed to Adelaide, where I'd had an offer from a fire brigade to speak to their staff and the local community about the journey I was on.

I'd never spoken in front of an audience before my kindness journey started—my first time was at that high school in Goulburn. So, I was a little apprehensive about this offer, which sounded quite corporate and serious to me, but I knew that South Australia would only add to what had already been an amazing experience. Plus, I knew a few people in other states who worked in fire services, so I was aware of how much they did for their communities, and I was proud to perhaps be able to offer something back to this group by sharing my story.

This engagement came as I approached one month away from home, although it seemed like about two years. So much had happened, and I felt completely changed as a person.

I got through the keynote presentation with relative ease, speaking from the heart in front of over 800 people. I was hugely surprised to receive a standing ovation, and I stood awkwardly, not knowing how to respond to such a generous gesture. Afterwards, a line-up of people wanted to talk to me, ask thoughtful questions and take photos. One of those people was Rachel.

You know how sometimes you meet people and you immediately feel a magnetic connection? That's how I felt with Rachel. She was stunningly beautiful, and had such a warm, feminine and soft nature that you just wanted her to give you a cuddle on the spot—which is what we did as soon as we'd introduced ourselves. We chatted for the next forty-five minutes or so, engrossed in our conversation. Finally Rachel and I said goodbye, but not before she handed me a twenty dollar note in case I ran into any trouble, and a business card with her number and address.

The chief firey was driving me to a hotel he'd booked for me that night, and on the way there I took out my phone to text Rachel my number and to say thanks for the chat. She responded immediately, inviting me to stay with her family for as long as I needed. She lived just north of Adelaide, which was convenient if I wanted to do anything in the city. Given that I'd made my debut for New South Wales at the Adelaide Oval, I was keen to get back there for a visit, and maybe catch up with some of the South Australian players I knew.

From my hotel room I gave Rachel a call to ask how she'd feel about me coming to stay for a few nights from the next day onwards. I had other offers to fall back on, but the exchange we'd had at the fire station was fresh in my mind. To be honest, I simply wanted to spend more time with her.

• • •

There were four beds in my unit at Royal North Shore. As you entered the room, I was in the far-left corner, and Jane was in the far-right corner—but, given the injuries we were both recovering from, we could only really stare at each other to pass the time. For the first few days I had my bed angled so that I didn't have to stare directly into her eyes, partly because it made me uncomfortable but also because I was trying to respect her privacy, and Jane was in a far worse state than I was, unable even to communicate her needs.

Jane had a brain injury: she was paralysed and almost completely immobile, apart from minimal use of her hands and arms. Jane's husband, Brian, came and visited her most days. I could tell that she looked forward to his visits, but apart from that, her only visitors were the medical practitioners who tended to her. As far as I could tell, Jane couldn't talk: she had daily speech therapy, which I couldn't avoid seeing and hearing.

I don't want to take away from the amazing work our health professionals do, and I appreciate the time pressures and staffing challenges they face in their work, but this particular speech therapist certainly lacked patience and empathy, in my opinion.

Brian and I sometimes said g'day and had a quick chat, and I learned from him that Jane had been the victim of a hit-and-run incident on a pedestrian crossing. She had been in hospital for several months already, and while her family had seen slight improvements, it had been a slog, to say the very least. This was clearly a lonely and uncertain time for Jane, and I often felt sad for her.

Friends of mine had put a schedule together so that I had a steady flow of visitors. While it was comforting to have that much support, I often craved quiet time, where I could give myself some rest and to not always have to put on a happy face. There was also a constant flow of gifts—chocolates, banana bread, flowers and balloons—for which I felt incredibly grateful, but I was never really sure what to do with it all.

One day, when the nurse asked me if there was anything I needed, I asked her to take the banana bread to the staffroom for their morning tea, but I also asked if she would take one of the bunches of flowers I'd received and put them in a vase for Jane. The nurse obliged, and as she came back with the flowers in water and a vase, she went to put them up on the shelf behind Jane.

'Any chance you could put them on the windowsill, in front of her?' I asked.

'Here?' she asked, pointing.

'Yeah, that would be great. Thanks so much for that.'

It was important to me that Jane could see the flowers as her own. I hoped she might take some comfort in them. While Jane had a brain injury and struggled to communicate, I could tell she knew what was going on. She turned her eyes to me, and the glimpse of a smile appeared on a corner of her mouth.

There weren't many things I could do from my hospital bed, especially in the early stages of my recovery, but making Jane smile at least once every day was something I could commit to. Not only might it help her recovery, but it gave me purpose every day. That's something we all need in life—a focus that gives us perspective and even, as I found, a brief distraction from the daily grind of recovery.

• • •

The thumbs-up is a common gesture of approval. After I met Jane, though, it took on so much more meaning for me—so much so that today, whenever I see someone giving a thumbs-up, I think of her.

Jane could understand verbal communication and body language and cues; she simply couldn't respond with words at this early stage of her recovery from brain injury. Sensing the frustration that she must have felt lying there day after day, I felt like everyone who was interacting with her needed to come up with creative ways to help Jane communicate without words.

As the hours and days passed in that hospital ward, and I watched Jane's recovery and worked on my own, I often wondered how different the patient experience would be if our health professionals prioritised emotional safety, trust building and kindness. And how different the health outcomes of those patients would be if these social and emotional skills were a key focus for our doctors.

Perhaps it was a resourcing problem—maybe our health professionals were simply too busy to slow down and consider the patient in front of them as more than their illness or injury. And I knew that neither Jane nor I would be afforded this kind of treatment in the high-risk ward that we were in, due to the demands and pressures on the staff: taking things slowly could literally mean life or death.

Beyond my own recovery, I had all the time in the world. I didn't want to interfere with Jane's treatment, but I also knew that I didn't need to be a doctor to make her smile—and I knew that would build trust and confidence, which I hoped might spur on her recovery. There's a lot to be said for having hope when you're in a hospital bed, and sometimes finding small moments of happiness could build that hope. I could sense that Jane wasn't feeling overly safe in the environment we were in, and that she needed a friend she could trust.

My own prognosis was a little unknown at the start. With multiple fractures in my spine and very limited movement in my legs, plus the added complexity of my first broken back, the doctors decided to spend some time seeing if my body would naturally start to heal itself. I was told to stay as calm as possible while waiting for swelling to ease, to see if my lower limbs would start to wake up. The waiting game was a difficult one for me. Short of staring at the ceiling or distracting yourself with your phone, there really isn't much in a hospital room to keep yourself occupied, and with no promises that the feeling in my limbs would start to come back, this extra time to think was not doing me any extra favours.

I'd just finished a physio session, which was far from what you might imagine. It consisted of me lying on my bed, with the physiotherapist moving my legs in a circle. By now you will understand that I'm an extremely stubborn person, and I spent most of the morning asking the physio to get me up and onto my feet. As I write that, I realise how crazy it sounds, but at the time I felt it was valid. I had to trust their process, but it was frustrating and slow.

I was self-aware enough to know that my lack of patience had started to show, and I asked the physio on this day if we could finish up early, citing my fatigue as an excuse.

I knew Jane had been watching—it would have been hard not to—but I also felt we had started to forge a bond, and I wanted to see if she might respond to me that afternoon. My bed was just at the right elevation for me to be able to see Jane without much effort, and Jane was in a similar position.

I tried just smiling at first, but I wasn't sure that she could see my face and read the non-verbal cue. Next I tried waving, but I soon got the impression that she was trying to avoid looking at me. I didn't want to give up, but soon enough it was visiting hours and Brian came in with a home-cooked dinner.

Jane was on a fluid-only diet, but bringing in his own meal meant they could eat together as husband and wife.

My attempts to make Jane smile again hadn't gone so well, but that didn't mean we hadn't taken a few steps forward. It would take time to build up enough trust, I knew, and I would have to be consistent in my efforts and in staying authentically myself.

• • •

Oliver and James are two of the most beautiful and well-behaved little boys I've ever met. Which shouldn't have surprised me, with a mum like Rachel. Anyone could have forgiven this beautiful family for being a little annoyed with me for showing up in their house—I was late, and it was well past the boys' bedtime—but they weren't.

Oliver and James were both still up, and were bunking in together in Oliver's room, so that I could have James's room. I heard giggling as I entered the warmth of Rachel's home.

'I don't suppose you would mind quickly reading the boys a bedtime story?' Rachel asked. 'They've been so excited to meet you! I've been talking about you all day.'

'Of course I'll read them a bedtime story—I would love that!'

I quickly met Rachel's husband, Max, then was taken through to see the boys. As I entered the bedroom, both of them vanished under the covers—and it reminded me of spending time with my nephews back home in Sydney, whom I was really missing. I pretended to look for them, feeling the covers for an arm or a leg to grab and tickle.

'Rachel, are you sure they're in here?' I asked. 'I can't see them . . . Oh, wait—I can feel something under here . . . Is that an arm?'

The laughter erupted from underneath the covers, and I looked up to see Rachel and Max smiling from ear to ear. I had only just met Max and Rachel the day before, and here I was reading their young children a bedtime story. It felt natural to me, as I'd done this so many times with my nephews and niece, but as I went to bed that night I wondered if I would be so trusting of someone I had just met.

In the living room, Max, Rachel and I sat next to their fireplace and chatted about life. It was important for me to set the foundation of our stay together by showing them who I was. I wanted them to know where I had come from, my beliefs and values as a person, and in turn I was keen for them to share this with me as well.

Trust has always been important to me. Without it I can't feel safe, and staying with strangers was uncertain enough. On the flipside, I knew Rachel and Max were taking a big risk in inviting a stranger to stay in their home. In sharing ourselves, we not only learned a lot, but our natural defences came down and we were able to be our authentic selves—which, I had come to learn, was a rarity in life.

I liked Max and Rachel, and was drawn in by their integrity and honesty. And that helped me trust them. When we are true to ourselves, as Max and Rachel are, not only do we trust the judgements and decisions we make but others trust us as well. Max and Rachel were people I could depend on, and I felt safe in their home.

• • •

The hardest part about being across from Jane was having to listen to her speech therapy sessions, which must have felt like torture for her. Her injuries were bad enough, and anyone could see that she was struggling, yet the therapist seemed to take a condescending tone towards her, which really annoyed me. I felt like Jane was being treated as anything but human in those moments.

Having gone through many hospital and rehab experiences already, I knew how detrimental moments like that could be on a person's morale, esteem and most importantly, their recovery. The kindness of others in allowing me to overcome the things that I had up until that point was very apparent throughout my journey and I knew it could have an impact on Jane as well, so long as she found those moments, and I felt it was up to me to be that person for her sometimes.

Other than Brian, who was a regular in our room, Jane didn't have much positive human interaction, and I could sense that his stamina was wavering as the weeks went by. Brian had noticed Jane's flower collection growing bigger by the day as I redirected half of what I'd been receiving towards her. I knew the people who were sending them to me would take just as much joy in Jane having them—plus I could still enjoy the hope and beauty that flowers can bring. I wasn't surprised when Brian thanked me for doing this for Jane—he seemed like a great bloke after all—but it did surprise me to see him welling up. He had to be weary from the four hours a day that he would commute just to see her. I so badly wanted to see her situation improve for the happiness of both of them, but I knew that every day was a battle.

One evening, my dad happened to be visiting at the same time as Brian, so I introduced them and they had a heart-to-heart chat in the corridor. I was glad that Brian could have a shoulder to lean on if he needed it, and my attention turned back to Jane. By this point I had started to regain some mobility, and I manoeuvred myself into the wheelchair beside my bed.

I edged myself over towards Jane's bed. There was a magazine on her meal table; I picked it up and made a joke about trashy magazines. No response from Jane. I worried that I had offended her, and went into chat mode to ease my own awkwardness.

'Jane, would you like me to read some of this to you?' I asked.

She nodded. Only very slightly, but it was a nod.

Twenty minutes later, Dad and Brian came back in, and were surprised to see me out of bed and reading to Jane.

'What are you two up to?' Brian asked.

'Just reading a magazine,' I said, before Dad wheeled me back to bed.

It was 8 pm and visiting hours were about to end. I propped myself back up in bed and noticed Jane staring at me. I gave her a thumbs-up and she smiled. My job was done!

From that time on, I read to Jane every day. Sometimes twice per day. When we weren't reading together, we were smiling and laughing at each other, and as her recovery started to improve, her smile became bigger and bigger, which was awesome to watch. She didn't share her smile with everyone, though—it was mostly just Brian and me. It was nice to be one of those people, but it also made me wonder what was going on for her. It wasn't my business to ask and, knowing the time that it took Brian to get to and from the hospital each day, I put it down to them being a little too far away for her normal supports to just drop in.

My biggest goal was to get her to give me a thumbs-up. She had always smiled the biggest when I'd sent one her way, so we worked hard at it every day, but she never quite managed it. Her injuries were so severe that even this small gesture was a huge challenge.

Jane's speech therapy was a very slow process, but it was coming on. I noticed that she had fewer words and less enthusiasm for the therapist than she did for me and Brian. I thought about this a lot and wondered why. We had been spending a lot of time together, but apart from our shared experience of injury and illness, we were strangers.

My health was definitely on the improve after a few weeks. I was no longer attached to cannulas and medical devices, and my increasing mobility saw me graduate from a chair to a walking frame. I still could not feel my left leg, but with the help of the frame I could get about alright. I still had a steady flow of visitors, so we'd go for a walk around the ward or down to the cafe for lunch. It felt great to be up and about, and that lifted my spirits higher than they'd been since my accident.

One day I was out of the ward for most of the day: I had some nerve tests in a different ward of the hospital in the morning, then physio in the afternoon, and then I headed down to the cafe for an early dinner with some friends. I was back in my bed by end of visiting hours at 8 pm, and exhausted from being out for the whole day. All I could think about was putting my head on the pillow and falling asleep.

As I walked past Jane on my frame, I was surprised to see that she was facing the other way. She must have heard me, I thought—my frame was loud and squeaky—so I guessed she was asleep. As I got into bed, I realised she was crying, her shoulders shaking as she tried to hold it all in.

'Jane, are you okay?' I asked. 'What's going on?'

She gave no response, so I got up again and moved across towards her. I put my hand on her shoulder, gently rubbing it to reassure her. Jane shrugged my hand off and, in the broken words she could manage, asked me to leave her alone.

I was crushed. Even though we only knew each other from this environment, I felt like we were friends. It hit me in that moment how much I cared for her.

I didn't sleep well that night. I hated knowing Jane was so upset about something, and I wanted to know why. Maybe I wanted to fix whatever it was, or maybe I just wanted her to know that I was there for her. I decided to follow up the next morning.

Breakfast was silent. We ate across from each other, and none of the jokes we had developed seemed to work anymore. Where had the smiles gone? After breakfast, I grabbed a magazine and asked if I could read to her. She shook her head.

Jane had speech therapy then, and I had physiotherapy, so I didn't see her again until the afternoon. Brian had arrived by this point, so I drew my curtain to give them some privacy. As I could hear him start to say his goodbyes, I put aside the book I'd been reading and got out of bed, walking outside our room intending to intercept him when he left. I didn't want to break Jane's confidence, but I wanted to see if Brian knew what was going on, and if there was any way I could help.

When he appeared, I spoke up. 'Brian, I'm worried about Jane. She hasn't been herself since yesterday. She won't talk to me or even let me read to her. Is everything okay?'

'Kath, Jane has the brain of about an eight-year-old now. She's improving, and we still have hope, but she has regressed.'

I understood what he was saying, but I couldn't figure out what that had to do with Jane's sudden change in her mood.

'You didn't read to her yesterday, did you?' Brian asked. 'Or visit? Or play games?'

He was right. I hadn't, and I felt terrible.

'Kath, you've been so good to Jane, doing everything you have. But she can't understand why you didn't do those things yesterday. I know it's not your fault—you have your own recovery to worry about, and a life to live. So please don't worry about this. It's my job to look after Jane.'

I felt absolutely shocking. I had let her down. Maybe Brian was right and I shouldn't have been so hard on myself for prioritising my own recovery, but that didn't mean it hurt any less to have let Jane down.

My discharge from hospital to the rehab unit was coming up, so I had two choices. I could accept that Jane was upset and leave her be, or I could try to explain what had happened and work towards regaining her trust.

I only had a couple of days, and I tried my best, but unfortunately Jane and I never really got back to where we had been as friends before I let her down. I know that her brain injury played a big role in our friendship breakdown, but I'm also sure that the break in consistency had a big impact. Consistency builds trust, and whenever I have been in positions like this since, and especially with kids, I make sure that I'm as consistent as I can possibly be. Because when trust is broken, it's hard to get back.

As I packed my bags and said my goodbyes to the other patients and the incredible staff who had kept me alive, I waved to Jane. She acknowledged me with a slight nod but nothing more, which made my departure a little sombre. After a few more goodbyes to my other roommates, I was on a hospital stretcher, ready to be transported to the rehab unit. The paramedics had just strapped me in tight, and I could barely move as they wheeled me out of our room and into the corridor.

We had almost reached the lift when a nurse came running down the corridor. 'Kath, come back! You have got to see this.'

'What?' I asked.

'It's Jane! Come back for a second!'

I looked at the paramedics with my most pleading eyes to ask the question, and soon enough we were heading back in the direction we'd just come from. I wasn't sure what I was going to see, but what I found gave me one of the most euphoric feelings of my life. Propped up on her bed, with her hand raised on a pillow, was Jane. She had got one of the nurses to help her form a thumbs-up. Not only that, but she was smiling as well.

It had taken her a few days to organise this with the nursing staff, I later learned, and required the assistance of Brian, who listened closely during their conversations each evening and passed on Jane's wishes to the staff.

• • •

I spent a few extra nights with Rachel and her boys, constantly in awe of the beautiful little family who took me in as one of their own, while planning my next move—on to Fremantle, Perth, to speak at another corporate organisation who had paid for my flights. The more time I spent with Rachel and the gang, the less I wanted to leave, as with almost every person I had met on the journey. What I learned with Rachel and the crew was not dissimilar to what I had learned through my connection with Jane—namely, that authenticity and consistency are the keys to establishing and maintaining trust. Without trust, we don't have safety. And safety in its various forms is a basic human need.

Humans are social beings. We crave connection and fear rejection. We can't have connection, certainly at a deep level, without trust. On the flipside, trust can help us form deeper interpersonal bonds. And with this can come an increased sense of optimism, higher levels of self-confidence, lower levels of stress and more meaningful social connections.

Think back to a time when you did not trust someone, for whatever reason. It's likely that person was less than honest about themselves or a particular situation. They may have tried to hide certain parts of themselves that they perceived to be faults or flaws, or they may have tried to devalue your input or worth. It is also very likely that your gut instinct was telling you to keep as far away from them as possible, or perhaps you just felt uncomfortable in their presence.

Trust is absolutely vital in our strongest relationships. Without it, we become less of ourselves, and we are unable to be kind to ourselves or others.

Humour

'Kath, really inspirational stuff. Love what you're doing. My mate Flippa reckons you'd have a few stories. Want to meet us for a beer?'

Never in my wildest dreams did I think that I'd make it all the way to Perth, but there I was, having finished the keynote for the company that flew me there with some time on my hands and many offers to help. I was close to six weeks into my journey, with about $60 in my pocket. My blog was being read by thousands of people around the world every day, and others were getting regular updates on the Kindness Factory's social media pages, which were now being followed by over 20,000 people.

Out of all of the offers that I received, this one—from someone calling themselves 'Gremlin'—had the most potential for fun. I gave Gremlin a call to see where she was, and it just so happened that she and Flippa were only about 800 metres from where I had just finished lunch. 'What time do you knock off from work?' I asked. 'I can come and meet you.'

'YOLO! We'll leave now. Meet us at the Imperial when you can!'

My journey to date had been powerfully sobering, and I was craving a fun experience, so I slung my backpack over my shoulders and walked a little faster than I had for a while. I had only been to this part of Australia once before, for a quick work trip, and I felt like a genuine stranger here.

I had no idea what Flippa and Gremlin looked like, but when I entered the pub I could have spotted them a mile away! Partly because it was 2 pm on a Tuesday and the pub was pretty empty, but also because with names like Flippa and Gremlin, I had a sneaking suspicion that they wouldn't take life too seriously.

'Girls, how are you?' I asked. 'Who's Flippa and who's Gremlin?'

After we'd made our introductions, Flippa asked, 'Can we get you a drink? What'll it be?'

'Whatever you guys are having would be great, thanks.'

Drinking was never really a big thing in my family. I could never tell you if I had a $10 or a $200 bottle of red in front of me, but I enjoy a drink and the way it loosens up a mood.

When I was in my late teens and early twenties, the majority of my friends were athletes like me, and we knew how to have a good time with or without alcohol—but when we did have a drink, we'd have stories to tell for years to come. I knew that having one or two with Gremlin and Flippa would lead to a few good laughs.

'Thanks for this,' I said when the drinks appeared. 'What did I end up with?'

'It's a Peroni,' said Flippa, but something about the way that she spoke, looking quickly at Gremlin with a half-smile, made me wary.

I took a sip. It didn't taste like beer, and there was a strong smell of alcohol coming from the neck of the bottle. 'Guys, what's in this? Is that vodka?'

Both of them erupted with laughter.

'I can't drink that!' I protested. 'I'll be ruined!'

Soon we settled into an easy conversation.

'Where are you off to next, Kath?' asked Flippa.

I wasn't exactly sure about that. I had an offer for a place to stay and dinner for that night, but it hadn't been confirmed yet. We chatted for the next couple of hours, not getting too over the top, and at around 5 pm I received a text from Tori, with the details of where I should meet her, her husband and another couple. I asked Flippa and Gremlin if they knew of the restaurant.

'It's right down the road, Kath—it'll only take you five minutes to walk there,' Gremlin said. 'What time is dinner?'

'I've got to be there for seven pm.'

'Plenty of time, then,' said Flippa, giving me a thumbs-up as she stood to head for the bar for another round.

'Nothing for me, thanks,' I said, wanting to be respectful of Tori and the others whom I would be joining that evening.

Moments later my phone rang. It was Tori, confirming the details and making sure I knew how to find them. I mentioned to Tori that I was with two friends, Flippa and Gremlin, and that I'd be leaving by 6.30 pm to meet her. But Gremlin grabbed the phone out of my hands and joined in with the conversation, inviting herself and Flippa along to dinner.

We all agreed that was fine, but I'd be lying if I said I wasn't nervous. I didn't know any of these people. I had spent a couple of hours with Gremlin and Flippa, and I'd never met Tori. I didn't even know the names of the other people who would be at dinner. It was one thing to ask each of these groups to accept me, but it was another to bring them together. I was struggling to see how everyone would get along.

As we walked towards the restaurant, I reminded both Flippa and Gremlin that I'd never met Tori and her friends, and I had no idea what they would be like. I half-wanted them to sober up a bit, but I was also reminding myself of their offer of help, so I was trying to be as respectful as I could to everyone. But after spending the afternoon together, I knew Flippa and Gremlin were really decent people. They had big personalities, but their humour aimed to make people smile, not bring anyone down.

So often we use humour to deflect attention away from hard topics or to stamp out vanity. Sometimes humour can be hurtful, and even lead to damaging outcomes. But this was not how Flippa and Gremlin were.

I once read a book called *The Choice*, written by a Holocaust survivor named Edith Eger. In it, she spoke about the difference between being childlike and childish. Being childish meant acting like a child and never growing up to own life's responsibilities. Being childlike, on the other hand, meant having a child's natural curiosity about life and a love for learning and discovery. When I was reading that book, I remember committing myself to always strive to be childlike in my thinking—to keep an open mind and to take a moment every day to laugh.

Life can often be awfully serious, and adversity happens to all of us, but we can always find an opportunity to find the lightness in life. Doing so is an act of kindness to ourselves and to the people around us. I respected that both Flippa and Gremlin seemed to do it quite naturally.

• • •

'Dawid, you have your shoes on the wrong feet again!'

I had just started my first rehab session in a shared physical therapy room, and Dawid was hard to miss. He was still in his pale blue striped pyjamas, and he was wearing the most immaculately shiny black shoes I had ever seen—but on the wrong feet. He either couldn't hear his physiotherapist half-talking, half-shouting at him, or he just didn't care.

'Dawid, come here. Gosh, they're not even tied up!'

I didn't expect to laugh a lot during my second stint at rehab. Knowing how tough it had been the first time, and with the reminder of everything I had lost at the front of my mind, I had been dreading it in the leadup to my transfer. As a result, I arrived with a lot of nervous energy.

My first night hadn't got off to a great start either. The patient transport vehicle had arrived late on a Friday, and we got stuck in peak-hour traffic, making an estimated 30-minute journey take close to two hours. By the time I arrived at the rehab facility, it was well past 6 pm. I hadn't made it in time for dinner, and I'd had a very near miss with the bathroom. On top of that, there wasn't the usual quota of staff, so I had to stay in my room instead of being given an induction, so I felt incredibly lonely.

The good vibes I had just experienced with Jane quickly vanished as my new reality became clear. In this new rehab environment, I had a lengthy recovery ahead of me. Ultimately, learning to walk again was going to be a huge challenge, given my prognosis and injuries. I didn't sleep much at all on that first night. The silence in my wing of the facility only added to the thoughts swirling around my mind.

The next morning, I met my assigned physiotherapist and had my induction tour—and then Dawid provided his very welcome distraction. There were a few things about him that grabbed my attention. He spoke in broken English—I tried hard to guess where his accent was from—and had a very quirky nature, and always wore a cheeky smile. Not long after Dawid sorted out his shoes, his therapist was on his case again, this time trying to stop him from using one of the balancing bars that another patient was working with.

That afternoon I saw Dawid again, this time in a new set of pyjamas. He was walking around the corridors whistling a song that sounded familiar to me, but I wasn't sure from where, so I stopped to ask him. He acknowledged me by nodding his head and smiling, and then he laughed in a way that suggested he was wishing me a good day. I couldn't tell if he was struggling to understand me or was working through a brain injury as many people in rehab were, but I smiled as I sat there in my wheelchair and watched him walk away from me. He had such a skip in his step that it was hard to believe he was in a rehab environment, and as he continued whistling I suddenly realised what song it was: 'Danny Boy'.

My mum's dad had always been a tough man. A typical
Aussie truckie, he smoked hard and drank hard, and his uniform
was a singlet, shorts and work boots. I remembered him whistling 'Danny Boy' in his shed of an afternoon. Although I had
no idea what the song meant, I suspected it had a significant
meaning, and hearing it here in rehab inspired me to look
it up.

I googled its origin and meaning, and read that the song was
a message from a parent to a son, wishing him a safe return
from war. The highest note, which soars up and ends on the
final note of 'come ye back', evokes a hope of meeting again.

Dawid had to be at least 85 years old, and I wondered if
he'd experienced war on the front line. It wasn't any of my
business to ask—we hardly knew each other. But I was fascinated by him.

Whenever I saw him in the next few weeks, he was always
wearing the same thing. Striped pyjamas, sometimes light blue,
sometimes dark blue. And he was always in his pristine black
shoes, ready to skip his way to wherever he needed to go next.
For the most part he kept to himself, and whatever it was he
was doing, he always found a way to laugh. It might have been
a session with his physio—Dawid would be in the water splash-
ing about and entertaining everyone. One day I saw him sitting
in front of a puzzle, almost talking to the pieces, and laughing
as if one of them had just said the funniest thing he'd ever heard.

A friend of mine, Nikki, came to visit one night, takeaway Thai food in hand to share with me for dinner. We went to the common area, where there were kitchen facilities, and sat at a table. It was quiet, and at first I thought we had the room to ourselves, but as we began our meal I noticed Dawid in a corner of the room.

Nikki and I hadn't caught up in quite a while, and we were soon absorbed in our conversation. Suddenly I realised Dawid had come towards us, with his usual beaming smile. Before I knew it he was standing so near to us that it made our conversation a little awkward—we felt like we were having a three-way chat now.

'Nikki, this is Dawid,' I said eventually. 'Dawid, this is one of my friends, Nikki.'

Nikki responded a little awkwardly. 'Nice to meet you, Dawid. How are you?'

He came closer still, as though he wanted to tell us a secret. But he mumbled something inaudible and then laughed, and that made both of us giggle, and soon all three of us were laughing uncontrollably. Once we'd got over this fit of the giggles, a few walls had been broken down and we engaged in a more normal conversation with our new friend.

There were two things Nikki and Dawid had in common. The first was that Dawid was in rehab recovering from a life-threatening heart attack—and Nikki was all too familiar with this, as she was a heart surgeon. The second thing was that both Dawid and Nikki were Jewish. Once we were chatting, it didn't take Nikki long to guess where he was from.

'Dawid, are you Polish?' she asked.

He nodded. 'From Krakow,' he said, and his smile vanished as he pulled down his pyjama sleeve, which had been rolled up.

Nikki chatted with Dawid about Judaism, which seemed to make him feel more comfortable, and his smile returned. I watched with fascination as the two of them interacted. Nikki is a shy person by nature, but that part of her personality retreated in Dawid's company.

'What did you used to do, Dawid? What was your job?' Nikki asked.

'Watchmaker,' he said, laughing.

I couldn't tell if he was joking or not. 'How did you get into that?' I asked.

He stopped laughing, looked me dead in the eye and said, 'I learned at Auschwitz.'

Both Nikki and I were stunned into silence, then I started fumbling around for words to fill the void. When I looked up at Dawid again, he was standing and removing his pyjama top to show Nikki and me the bullet holes in his back, and the faded but legible tattoo on his arm, which only moments earlier he had wanted to keep hidden.

I was blown away that the shiny-shoed man before us—who was possibly the most cheerful man I'd ever come across—had endured one of the most horrific places on Earth. My mind was spinning. I couldn't even begin to imagine what he had been through—which made it all the more impressive that he was able to smile and laugh each day. I didn't know how he did it, but what I did know was that I wanted to spend more time around him.

Dawid became my new best friend in rehab, a person with whom I'd spend the next few months laughing and learning. Friends could be hard to find in rehab, but much like Whip did, Dawid kept me grounded and in the moment. Acknowledging this while it was happening was new for me, and I realised that my self-awareness was improving with age and experience.

• • •

At the restaurant, we made our introductions and ordered, but the mood was a little awkward. We were seven strangers, and how we all had come to be there together was rather odd. Our interactions felt a little stiff at the start as a result. Tori and her friends were all from the corporate world, and were well dressed and very well spoken. I was wearing a pair of dirty white Converse sneakers and a hoodie that was in need of a wash, while Flippa's and Gremlin's carefree natures were a little loud at first.

It wasn't long before Flippa broke the tension with a joke, which everyone appreciated. That was when the penny dropped for me that humour can be different things to different people. But the way Flippa and Gremlin used it would change the way I thought about humour and laughter forever.

No one wants to be the butt of someone else's joke. The brutality of that type of humour can be very detrimental to a person's self-esteem. But when humour is used in an inclusive way, or to break the tension during a conflict, it can have very positive impacts on people's lives.

One of Tori's friends, Nadia, was Latin American and didn't speak much English. After I introduced Flippa and Gremlin, all the Australians around the table laughed at their nicknames. Nadia, however, had not understood what we were all laughing at. I know Flippa noticed this too, as she turned her attention towards her.

'Nadia, how would you say this in Spanish? F L I P P A,' she spelled out, slowly but respectfully.

Nadia translated—simply repeating the word with different intonation—and the table again erupted with laughter. Nadia shrugged, a grin on her face. 'Okay how do you say this?' Flippa lifted her phone to show a photo of a gremlin, which she had just googled.

Nadia provided the Spanish translation—*duendecillo*—and the table laughed again. And for the rest of the evening, everyone called Flippa and Gremlin by their new Spanish nicknames.

The very clever way Flippa had used humour to include Nadia, after noticing she was feeling left out, was wonderful. Indeed, when it's paired with empathy and humility, humour can be one of the best and safest ways to showcase kindness. Humour helps us connect with other people—joy and laughter truly are the foundations of good human relationships.

• • •

After that night with Nikki and Dawid, we became pretty inseparable. The common room became our meeting place for lunch each day, and in the evening it was where we laughed and talked and shared our experiences.

What Dawid had endured was the furthest thing from funny, but that didn't stop him from seeing the lighter side of life whenever we were together. Dawid was good for me, and I looked forward to spending time with him. I learned more of his past, and the horrific nature of what occurred at Auschwitz, which shocked and saddened me. It wasn't Dawid's favourite subject, but it was important to him.

I knew Dawid volunteered with various Jewish organisations, sharing his story with strangers, and I wondered how this had impacted him emotionally. Sharing my story of trauma and adversity was always a big drain on me emotionally, and I hadn't been through half of what Dawid had. And he told his story with nothing removed, the cruelty of his captors explored in detail. He didn't do this for pity, or to win praise, but because he believed that talking about such atrocities would shock people. It did do that, no doubt, but Dawid hoped that shocking audiences in this way would prevent such barbarism from ever happening again.

Dawid's humour always kept him upbeat. If you didn't know him or his background, you could honestly have mistaken him for the happiest man in the world. He whistled wherever he went, he walked with a skip in his step, and he was always laughing. Dawid used humour in a charming way that made people feel safe. He was never offensive; if he was ever making fun of someone, it was usually himself.

Dawid paired humour with perspective. He had seen the very worst of humanity at a young age, so it was important for him to balance those awful experiences with as much goodness as possible. He chose to do this by smiling as much as he could.

The best lesson I learned from Dawid was that laughter was a choice. He didn't wake up every day with a magical ability to find happiness. He made an active decision to be the way he was. He made me see that I too had that choice. We all do.

• • •

We laughed the night away as Flippa and Gremlin regaled us with stories of their antics. The drinks kept flowing, and at one point I could tell that the alcohol had started to get the better of Gremlin.

'Tracey, thanks so much for having Flippa and me join you tonight,' she said, looking at Tori. 'It's been a real treat.'

We were all a little confused, and Tori didn't reply.

Gremlin looked across at her again, making eye contact so there was no confusion. 'It really was a pleasure, Tracey, thanks.'

Tori looked confused. 'Me?' she asked.

Before anyone could say anything, Tori stood up then walked around the table and put her arms around Gremlin's shoulders. 'It's been great to meet you too, Gina!' she said. 'But my name is Tori!'

They both laughed, and the rest of us joined in. Rather than taking offence at Gremlin's misunderstanding, Tori had joined in the fun, making fun of herself in the process, which only intensified the group's laughter. I was pleased that I had brought this group of people together, and even more pleased when they all exchanged numbers at the end of the night.

When Tori, her husband and I were in the car on the way home, she thanked me for a wonderful night.

That made me stop in my tracks—if there was anyone who should be thanking someone, it was me! With the help of humour, we had shared kindness as well as dinner and drinks that night.

Honesty

I've always found kids to be honest and straightforward, which is probably why I like hanging around them so much. You never have to guess what they're thinking. So speaking to some students at a primary school in Brisbane was incredibly refreshing. My time in Perth had been relatively short, especially considering the distance I'd travelled to get to the west of the country and then back to the North East. I'd made my way to Queensland after accepting an invitation from someone within the Queensland Department of Education, who also offered to put me up for as long as I needed in their family home.

The Brisbane kids I found myself in front of were between eight and twelve years old, so I tailored my story in an age-appropriate way. I spoke about my love of cricket, and what it was like playing for New South Wales; how injury had changed my life, but not necessarily in a bad way; the importance of having good friends; and of course, my belief in the power of kindness.

Having been a pretty active aunty for a decade by then, I had a bit of experience communicating with kids, so I felt at home in front of them. But I knew it was important to include them in the conversation, so they didn't get too restless or bored.

'Any questions, guys?' I asked.

Pretty well all 300 kids shot up their hands.

I invited a little boy in the front row to ask his question.

'How long have you been going for?' he asked.

'Mmm, I think it's been about seven weeks now,' I responded, almost surprising myself. Next I pointed to a little girl to my right, who was waving at me excitedly.

'Are you a vegetarian?' she asked.

I was a bit puzzled as I hadn't spoken about that.

'I'm a vegetarian,' she went on. 'It's kind to animals.' Then she smiled up at me, and I knew she had been listening after all.

'I'm a vegetarian too,' I said, smiling back at her.

'Are you still sad?' asked a voice from the back of the room.

I looked around, trying to spot who had asked the question, and a little boy raised his hand. 'Why do you think I'm sad?' I asked him, moving closer so that I could properly engage in the conversation.

'It's just . . . you look a little sad.'

Now I had to think on the run. My journey had taught me so much about myself: perspective and trust, gratitude and humility, and much more besides. I had received so much kindness to date, but could I honestly say that I wasn't sad? I couldn't. The truth was that I had been through a lot in life, and I would carry the weight of those experiences with me forever. That didn't mean I would never find happiness again, just that I had a way to go before it could balance out the sadness I still felt sometimes.

It was important to me that I was honest with these kids, but I also wanted to explain that sadness was a healthy emotion, and one we shouldn't run from. I thanked the boy for his question and then answered him.

'You know what? I am a little bit sad sometimes, just like all of us can be—for many different reasons, I think. I miss what I used to be able to do a little bit. I love what I do now, and this trip I'm on has allowed me to meet some amazing people . . . But I think I'm starting to miss my friends and family a little bit too. Maybe it's time for me to go home again soon. What do you guys reckon?'

More hands shot up. 'Maybe if you're sad, you could tell someone that you trust that you're sad,' one kid said.

I nodded and smiled. As adults, we tend to dismiss a lot of what children say, but the more time I spend with them, the more I've realised how right they usually are.

I answered questions for the next half an hour or so, until finally the school bell rang. It was 3 pm and their parents would be coming to pick them up soon. I was invited into the staffroom for afternoon tea, and there I got chatting to some of the teachers about what had just happened. I think they too wanted to know if I was okay. The truth was I was 100 per cent okay. I had found a way to sit with the enormity of life and not have to run from my negative emotions anymore.

We all feel sadness at times, and that's okay. But the answer I'd given the kids was an honest one. Was I feeling sadness because of my past, or was I missing my home, my family and my friends? I didn't know.

I gave Erin a call, and when she asked how I was, I surprised myself by saying I was nearly ready to head home. It wasn't that I wasn't having a great time, I explained, but I was getting tired of living day to day and having to organise everything to the minute. Erin, as usual, was completely straight with me in return, and I hung up feeling clear and focused. I would see how I felt over the next few days and make a decision about my next move based on my gut feeling, which had never led me astray. Wherever the journey took me next, I would be content.

• • •

The period after leaving rehab and adjusting back to 'normal' life is a tricky one. On the one hand you're stoked to be well enough to be at home again, but on the other hand, it's a pretty vulnerable time, even when you have wonderful support people around you.

I was by no means back to 100 per cent when I left rehab after my cycling accident. I still needed crutches to get around, and my release was dependent on me being able to stay with support people and in a home that had no stairs. My only real option was to stay with one of my brothers, Craig and his family, which meant I had the company of my six-year-old and four-year-old nephews, Max and Sam, whenever they weren't at school.

That kept me distracted from my outpatient schedule, and from the reality that my mental health had started to decline. When Max and Sam were around, I could focus on them rather than on the emotions that had started to consume me every day. I longed for a simpler life—one that wasn't as much of a burden on me, but also, and more importantly, on those closest to me.

The more I pushed my emotions aside, hiding them behind humour and a smile, the harder it became for me to manage them. If Max and Sam weren't there to play Ninja Turtles with me, or if I wasn't at a rehab or medical appointment, I was left to my own devices. That was almost torturous, because my mind inevitably took me to parts of my life that still haunted me. The words left unsaid around Jim's passing, the injuries I still had to overcome, and the amount of support I required from family and friends created a constant swirl of noise in my mind.

I was 28 years old, and my Facebook and Instagram reels were full of old schoolfriends and others of a similar age who had their life in order—everyone was buying houses, getting married and having children. And here I was, living in my brother's granny flat and barely able to walk. I had got way ahead of myself, I now saw. I often cried myself to sleep, only to wake up the next morning and have to grind through another day.

My outpatient recovery felt painfully slow, and the more I tried to hurry it along, the harder life became. Then, not long after I was discharged, Wendy passed away.

It was a loss that came out of nowhere. It tortures me still to acknowledge that Wendy's death was a result of suicide too. I knew that Wendy had been struggling since we lost Jim, but I had always thought it was a load we would continue to carry together. The suddenness of her passing left me feeling lost and numb, and without the other person who knew Jim best I felt completely alone in my grief. I didn't blame her or feel any resentment towards her—I couldn't imagine the pain of losing a child—but I did wonder how I was going to process a loss as big as this without the person who had helped me get through the grief of losing Jim. Although my body was still in a bad way, I got myself up to the Gold Coast. On crutches and heavy pain medication, I wept through another funeral service marking a life gone too soon.

I was broken. Not only had I just lost an important person from my life, but Wendy was my last real connection to Jim. In some ways it felt like I had lost him all over again. Wendy's passing would have shaken me deeply even without everything else that was going on. I felt like everyone was seeing the cracks that were starting to appear in my life, and I made the mistake of trying to mask them so as not to alarm anyone.

My brother Grant had just become a dad to my beautiful nephew Andy, who was born on the day Wendy died, which was a reminder to me of the beauty and brutality that life could bring, all in the one day. For my family and for me, Andy's birth was the wonderful news we all needed.

Things in my life were moving too quickly for me to process them properly. Before my accident, I had been looking to purchase an apartment, going as far as gaining a pre-approved loan with a bank, and, now in recovery, when one came up that I liked, I impulsively decided to buy it. Perhaps I was trying to regain some control in my life—to pretend that I was still on the same track that I'd been on before breaking my back for a second time.

While it was on the ground floor—a necessity for me with my new mobility issues—and close to my family in Mortdale, I had overreached. I'd never lived alone before. I'd never had a mortgage before. And I was in a different financial situation now. One day I got a letter that said the third-party insurance I had might not cover my hospital, rehab and medical bills. A legal process was set to begin, but having signed up to a very large mortgage, it's safe to say I was more than a little stressed about money at that point, which meant that I returned to work a little earlier than what I was prepared for. I was, of course, physically cleared as safe to start transitioning back to the office, but again, in hindsight—I probably wasn't emotionally prepared for such a big load with everything else that had been going on.

On a long weekend in June, about five months after my accident, I invited some close friends around to see my new place and help me christen it with some food and drinks. One drink became a few, and soon enough we were all on our way, with music blaring and drinking games in full swing.

I shouldn't have been drinking at all—I was still on light medications, and I knew it wouldn't end well—but I was in the company of friends and wanted to forget my worries and have a bit of fun. The night ended with me in tears, and five or six of my friends seeing the anguish that had been building up within me since my accident.

After putting me to bed, they let themselves out, and the next morning I woke up to a text from each of them to see if I was okay. Not wanting to alarm anyone, I lied and told them I was fine. I was also trying to fool myself, I now see. Had I been honest with myself, I could have saved myself a whole lot of turmoil before getting the help that I needed. Even then, I think I knew I would reach my breaking point soon enough.

I had received a flurry of bottles of wine and spirits from friends and family, congratulating me on my new home. I don't know why I thought it would be a good idea to try them, especially on weeknights, but it became a habit to pour myself a drink after work or rehab. It was a way for me to escape my feelings. Most nights I'd end up passed out on the couch, not having eaten but having drunk plenty. I'd wake up the next morning, shower and promise myself I wouldn't do it again—only to finish whatever I was doing in the afternoon and then start the cycle again. I wanted to forget about my worries, but I also felt real sadness for my old life. And living by myself had thrown me into a solitary silence that I was uncomfortable with.

I didn't see all of this as a big problem at the start, but slowly my closest friends noticed the cracks appearing in my life. One of those friends was Erin.

As I've mentioned before, Erin is the most consistent person I know. She always shows up and she always knows what to do. I knew she would see through my smile and have a tough and honest conversation with me, which was what I needed. So, shamefully, at certain times I avoided her. I cancelled plans we made at the last minute, I'd be slow to respond to texts, and if she called I would text her to say that I was at work or rehab, or out to dinner with family.

Erin could easily have just got on with her life. She deserved better from me. She had never once turned her back on me, and the least I could do was to try to get my life back on track.

I'd begun socialising with people who encouraged my new-found interest in drinking and partying, which was out of character for me. I was out one night with a new friend from this group, having a few drinks not far from Erin's place. As the evening progressed, Erin happened to call me, so I picked up and invited her to join us. She was excited to see me when she showed up twenty minutes later. But I was six beers in and sloppy, almost collapsing into her arms as she gave me a long and overdue hug.

I sensed her concern for me, and tried to avoid it by going to the bar to order us all a drink. Soon enough she'd convinced me to call it a day, and we walked back to her place, where she put me to bed, promising to take me home in the morning. It was a Sunday night and I had work the next day, so we were up early. As she dropped me off at home, she gave me a hug, looked me in the eye and told me she would be in touch in the afternoon to see how I was.

I had a first-aid course at work that day, and I was far from my best, taking regular breaks outside in between completing breaths and compressions on a mannequin. We wrapped up the session early, which I was grateful for—I desperately needed an early night.

On the train home, as a sad song played on my headphones, I took a few deep breaths, feeling like I was sinking towards rock bottom again. My eyes welled up when I thought about how hard I had worked to get through everything after breaking my back the first time and here I was, my body broken again, having lost my last connection to Jim in Wendy, and drinking my life away.

At that moment I received a text from Erin. I still have that message saved in my phone—it reminds me of the immense power of friendship, but also that I have people in my life who will always show up for me, regardless of how hard the situation is.

Erin's words were honest and direct. It was hard for her to watch me throw my life away, she said, but that's what it looked like I was doing. To see that spelled out so bluntly was a real wake-up call. But what Erin wrote next had me swiping tears from my cheeks—she would be there to support me, no matter what.

Sometimes the most potent form of kindness is a healthy dose of honesty. I'd been lying to myself, pretending I was fine, but her text made me see what was really going on. Her honesty in that moment gave me clarity—she was able to put into words the immense burden of life that I was carrying, and her words enabled me to begin to share just how hard the past six months of my life had been.

I got off the train and called Erin as soon as I had some privacy. I didn't want her worrying about me a moment longer, and I felt ready to start talking. I believe it was as I heard myself telling her what I was feeling that I started to heal. It allowed me to start to find compassion and acceptance for myself, which is where I needed to begin.

I once heard someone say that we learn how we feel when we say it aloud, and I've found that to be true. The longer I talked with Erin about how I was feeling, the easier it was to find empathy for myself.

If a friend of mine talked about themselves the way that I was, I would absolutely tell them to be kinder. So why wasn't I affording that same compassion, empathy and kindness towards myself? When the truth was laid out in front of me like that, in a raw and honest way, I started to see things clearly again. My physical and emotional recovery was a choice. I could choose to continue struggling alone, or I could accept the readily available support of my family and friends, who would help me get my life back on track—whatever that looked like.

HONESTY

• • •

After my conversation with Erin on my way home from work after first-aid training, I felt able to start accepting more help from friends and family. I also started seeing a wonderful psychologist, who began to open up my world in a very gentle way. The barriers I had created for myself in not accepting help—and in refusing even to acknowledge that I needed it—were plentiful.

Cricket is a male-dominated sport, even for kids at a young age and especially when I was a little girl growing up playing in the local boys' competition. Thankfully for me, having three older brothers helped protect me from the teasing that would pop up from time to time if you were seen to be outperforming any of the boys on the opposing teams. Before I'd even walked out onto the field, therefore, I felt I had something to prove. 'Girls don't belong in boys' sports,' some said; I was taking the place of a boy who could have played. Being exposed to these attitudes built a grittiness in me—I wanted to prove them wrong and not show any weakness.

For most of my life, I hadn't let myself be different from the person everyone thought I was. As I took stock now, I saw that if I was to find happiness again, or even the real me, I needed to honestly examine who I was and how I saw my life. I had so often been labelled as resilient by people just for not giving up, and I'd never felt comfortable with that title. Being perceived as resilient is not something I'm overly proud of, because I think it leaves less room for me to be myself in the moment. It also meant that I felt pressure to overcome things in a superhuman way, without honestly experiencing the emotion of whatever it was I was undergoing.

When I was struggling, I often felt like I was in the trenches. I was surviving, but only just. I would tell myself, 'Just get through today—tomorrow will be better' or 'If I can just get through today, then tomorrow I'll do something about the pain I'm feeling. Just not today.' I was living in survival mode, and that meant I found it extremely hard to make an objective assessment of how I was really going. My ego prevented me from being vulnerable enough to simply say, 'I need help.' What I know now is that being truly honest with yourself requires radical self-acceptance.

Erin has always been a beacon of light for me. Because of who she is, she was able to have the hard and honest conversation with me that she did. Yes, it was uncomfortable for both of us. It could easily have gone wrong—I could have interpreted her intervention as judgemental. I definitely wasn't ready to hear what she was saying. But Erin didn't have to fix what I was going through. Maybe it couldn't have even been fixed.

Being honest with myself each day—even when it's just about the little things in life—is important. Life isn't black and white. One thing I've always struggled with is saying no. I don't like letting anyone down, but agreeing to everything can leave little space for the things and people I really enjoy. When considering new opportunities and requests, I have to ask myself: 'Is this me just not wanting to say no, or is this something that is important to me?' More often than not, I am able to have an honest conversation with myself about how to respond. In doing this, I am choosing momentary discomfort over later resentment. It's a form of self-kindness.

We don't need to wait until our difficulties are affecting all facets of our life before we acknowledge that we are 'not okay'. These days I ask myself: *What area of my life could I benefit from addressing today?* Because there are always areas in our life that could use a bit of tweaking here or there and because none of us are perfect.

• • •

I left the school in Brisbane after spending the afternoon with most of the teaching group who'd invited me. I was now seriously considering my next move. I had constantly been learning on this journey, and this school experience with the students and the teachers was no exception to that. Since leaving high school eleven years prior to the journey that

I was on, I really hadn't given schooling or even more broadly, education as a whole, any great deal of thought. Sure, I had teacher friends who would tell stories of what it was like to be in front of kids every day, but I really had no grasp of the challenges that children faced on a daily basis. What I learned through the teaching group on that day, and have continued to learn over the six years since, was that the mental health of kids was on a rapid decline, and there wasn't enough happening in the preventative mental health space for them to be able to do anything about it.

It had me baffled to even think about myself in the school yard all those years ago—I was already in my senior year in high school by the time mobile phones started to creep in. I had a Nokia brick phone that could dial and receive calls; text messages were tapped out using the digits on the phone itself, and most importantly, it had a game of snake on it, which most kids today would think was pretty primitive compared to the graphics on their iPhones. These days, I've been told that our access to technology means human beings have the opportunity to learn more in one day than what our great grandparents did in their entire lifetime. I don't blame technology for the mental health crisis, but if I found it easy to end up in an endless scroll as an adult, surely our kids with their sponge-like brains must be feeling pretty overstimulated too? I'm certain that that school in Brisbane was where the idea

was first planted within me to create the Kindness Curriculum, which has now been rolled out in thousands of schools
in three countries.

I knew I was nearing the end of my journey, but after the
experience I'd had with the kids at the school, I wasn't quite
ready to go home. Almost, but not quite. As I headed back to
my base for the evening, I swiped through my inbox, looking
over the offers from people around the country. My eye
snagged on one from members of an Indigenous community
in Darwin, and, clicking through, I decided that this would be
the perfect next step.

Compassion

Once I'd decided to head to Darwin, I made a few calls. I had plenty of offers of accommodation, and there would be many people to meet, but I didn't know how I would get there. I shared my problem on the Kindness Factory's social media pages, which were growing with followers by the minute, as everyone tried to keep up with where I was and how I was tracking. I offered my services in case that was appealing to anyone: in exchange for a bus ride, a plane fare or a train ticket, I would happily speak at a workplace or school. Or if anyone had any creative ideas to get me there, I said, I was open to hearing them.

Soon enough I was invited to speak at a company lunch, put on by two neighbouring businesses who came together to fund my airfare. After sharing my journey at the lunch, I made my way to a few neighbouring schools to share my experiences, give some perspective and amplify the power of human kindness. I loved the feeling of the air in Darwin, which at times reminded me of my carefree days in Finley. Home was calling me at every opportunity, I realised, which was a good feeling. I was starting to really miss the people who I loved the most.

Up to that point in my life, I hadn't spent much time with anyone from an Indigenous community, apart from a few friends from school and through cricket. And as a white woman who has benefited from my privileged position, I knew there were many elements of the Indigenous experience that I didn't understand. But I was keen to learn, and my kindness journey seemed exactly the right time to attempt to do so.

The day after I arrived in Darwin, I connected with a community group that a family I'd met in Melbourne put me in touch with. One conversation led to another, and soon I found myself meeting Aunty Meg, who not only agreed to take me in for as long as I needed it, but also to introduce me to her family.

Aunty Meg had done her research on me, and told me she thought I needed perspective. She didn't say this in a condescending way at all—it was more along the lines of, 'Come to my neck of the woods, we'll sort you out. You don't seem too bad for a white sheila.' Tone is everything in conversations like this, and she had a wise and endearing voice so I felt safe.

Aunty Meg drove me to a women's shelter she ran. I wasn't allowed to know its location, and I had to sign a confidentiality agreement—and, of course, Aunty Meg had sought the permission of the guests who were using the facilities. When she told me this was what she had planned, I was immediately drawn to the idea. Naturally, I was upset by the idea of women and children struggling, but I wanted to help in whatever way that I could.

The guests' safety was of course the top priority, but I'd be lying if I said it didn't make me nervous to be blindfolded during the journey there. I felt vulnerable, and tried to make small talk with Aunty Meg as she drove. She squeezed my knee a couple of times, trying to ease my nerves.

When she told me I could remove the blindfold, I fumbled with my sweaty hands to take it off. We walked towards the back door of the facility, which was neatly kept. It was a very simple set-up, but you could tell the place was well looked after. A whiteboard in the first common area of the house assigned chores and responsibilities to each of the guests. They had all assumed pseudonyms at the shelter, which were on stickers on their shirts, but most guests seemed to keep to themselves.

The rooms all had bunk beds. When a woman had children with her, they were prioritised for a private room. The largest room, which wasn't very large at all, had eight bunks in it, and could house twenty people at capacity, with smaller children sleeping with their mothers.

The guests all seemed very respectful of each other's situation. This was a safe place, well organised and running like clockwork. At first I felt it lacked character and love—but I was wrong.

A therapist was there during business hours to offer emotional support to the guests if they needed it. These sessions were held in a room towards the front of the house, which also housed a desk for Aunty Meg and her administrative helper, Danni. Aunty Meg knew all the women and children by name, and really engaged with them whenever they talked. She treated them with great dignity, and spoke with clarity and care. She reinforced this with a gentle shoulder rub or hand squeeze, and she never hurried them along, even though, as I knew from shadowing her, she had a thousand things to do.

I could tell that the women and children adored Aunty Meg. Most of the time the women kept their eyes turned to the floor, but if Aunty Meg was in the room, their attention was on her: they wanted to take in everything she was saying. The longer I watched, the more I was in awe of Aunty Meg and what she was doing for these families. She was literally saving their lives.

We ate lunch together, and then I was invited to a group therapy session—the caveat being that anyone who was in the session had to participate. For everyone to truly feel safe, it was important that we all took our armour off and were vulnerable together.

First we introduced ourselves, and I was the only person who didn't have to hide my identity. It struck me again how privileged my life was. When I chose to go back to Sydney, I knew, my apartment would be waiting for me. And all I had to do, if I was ever feeling lost or unsafe, was call one of my family members or friends, and I knew they would drop everything and run to me. Not everyone in our society can say the same—I was incredibly fortunate.

After introductions, the therapist turned to me. 'Welcome to the group, Kath. It's nice to have you join us. What's on your mind today?'

I felt like a complete fraud sitting next to these incredibly strong and beautiful people, and I told them so. When I spoke about my background and what I was doing, my face went red. I was completely embarrassed. Why had thousands of people reached out to help me, while these women were struggling alone in such desperate situations? I wasn't any better or braver than them, and I certainly hadn't endured more than they had. Just like Jessie in Melbourne, these women deserved love— as we all do.

Our circumstances were very different, and I knew that adversities shouldn't really be compared. For these women, maintaining privacy was the top priority, so they couldn't do something public like I was doing, but that prompted me to wonder where their support networks had been. Yet I was naive in thinking this way. I had no experience of the complexities of domestic violence, and it wasn't always just physical abuse. I decided to listen with openness and empathy, and learn from them.

It was extraordinary to listen as these women shared their lives with the group. I've never witnessed such bravery, before or since. It was one thing for them to have found this safe haven, but it was another to talk openly about their experiences, in the hope of healing. The women who spoke to the group that afternoon were afforded the utmost respect, dignity and compassion. If one of them was struggling, it meant that they all struggled together. If one of them laughed, they all laughed together. They were a family, brought together not by blood but by circumstance and choice.

I wanted to stay longer—which Aunty Meg had predicted. Spending time with these women wasn't draining or difficult, which I'd half-expected it to be, given all they had been through. But I realised then that this wasn't a domestic violence shelter—it was a home. It was Aunty Meg's home, and everyone who needed a place was welcome.

When Aunty Meg and I left, we drove in silence. I had to put my blindfold back on for the first part of the trip. I would have kept it on longer—the more I had come to understand of the women's situations, the more I wanted to protect their privacy—but Aunty Meg insisted that I should remove it after ten minutes or so.

'Aunty Meg, do you take many people to the shelter?' I asked as I put the blindfold back into the glovebox in front of me.

'Not many. Just the ones who need it.' She was smiling as she spoke.

I was a little confused.

'You have a family,' she told me. 'They're all waiting for you back at home. They're probably worried sick that an old black lady has kidnapped you in the NT! Go home, Kath. Let them all in.'

I knew exactly what she meant. I'd begun this journey in search of something, but I realised now that everything I needed was there in the people who had always shown up for me. My blood family, but also the family of friends who had always been there for me. As much as I felt drawn to return to the women's shelter to help however I could, another part of me was telling me to go home and to hug my people tightly. Kindness and human connection can be found anywhere—as I knew from experience.

• • •

Seven months after my accident, and following Erin's guidance to help me get back on track, I spent almost four weeks on her red futon couch. I had acknowledged that being on my own would not get me through. I had been discharged from rehab, but I was still a long way from being fully recovered.

Erin showed me compassion on a new level as I slowly started to find my feet again. It was one thing to help me realise I needed help, but true compassion requires action. Erin became an active participant in my recovery, keeping me company, checking in with me and giving me a home when I didn't feel as though my own company was enough.

It was wonderful to have someone to bounce things off again. I had spent so long trying to cope by myself that Erin's support almost felt foreign to me. I had spoken to my boss about having some more time away from my role at Cricket NSW. My workplace had been incredibly generous in giving me the time off that I needed to heal physically, and now I was asking for more time off—but I was met with compassion and understanding. That was an incredible privilege, and one that not everyone is lucky enough to enjoy.

Living at Erin's, I felt like I slowed down enough to start breathing properly again, for the first time in what had been a tumultuous period. Suddenly, everything started to become clearer, and I began feeling more like my old self—which was a huge relief to me.

Something I didn't anticipate, though, was having to go to court and face the man who had hit me with his car. I had never been involved in a legal process like that, so the idea made me nervous, even though I knew I hadn't done anything wrong. Every time my phone rang, I felt as though I was in trouble—the man's legal team was fighting the charges he'd been given after the collision.

It was expected to be a three-day hearing. On the first day, the man did not even show. This irritated me like I didn't know was possible. I am not someone who angers easily, but as I was being updated on the phone by the police, I couldn't help but let a bit of that frustration creep into my voice. I was shocked to learn that the police had also made a huge error in processing the charges throughout the court process. I had fractured my wrist and broken my back in four places, and my neck is still compromised as a result of that accident; yet the charges reflected the equivalent of a papercut. This didn't mean that justice wouldn't be carried out; it had been proven that the driver was at fault undeniably. My dad, who had been a police officer for forty years, was appalled by the error—we both tried to explain the mistake, but I felt completely dismissed by the police officer we were dealing with. To add insult to injury, I had to take off yet another day of work to appear in court as a result of the error, in order to meet the judge face to face. I hate the word victim, as I feel it diminishes the person going through an injustice even more. But if there was a victim in all of this, it was me, and yet here I was, still in the midst of my physical and mental recovery from this accident, dealing with the additional stress that the justice system was layering on top of that. That police officer made me feel like I was the one on trial, which made the process even more traumatic than it should have been.

On the second day of court, we learned the severity of the punishment that the driver was facing; and on the third day, those punishments were handed down to him. When he heard the sentence, he broke down in tears, his head in his hands.

My heart sank for him. I wasn't surprised by the result of the hearing, with the process now having been taken over by the judge and legal process, but I was shocked by my own response to seeing him so upset. I genuinely felt for him. I've been an empathetic person since childhood, and I just couldn't ignore this man who was so upset.

I knew he had not set out to hurt me that day. He had made a mistake, and I had been harmed, but it was not intentional. It hurt me that he had not attempted to contact me after the accident to see if I was okay—but perhaps his legal team had instructed him not to.

We all make mistakes. I make at least ten per day. Thankfully for me, most of my mistakes don't have as big an impact as this man's did.

Feeling overwhelmed by the proceedings, I had positioned myself at the back of the courtroom. I was surprised to hear the judge ask me to stand so he could address me. I rose nervously, thinking I was about to get in trouble for something. But the judge simply looked at me and apologised profusely for the error in processing that was made by the police officer. This incredibly simple gesture by a very well regarded judge shifted the entire experience for me. I felt like a human being again, which is something we should all be afforded, victim or not. Compassion is in the thinking, feeling, but most importantly, it's in the doing. When the judge issued this apology in front of that courtroom of people, she allowed me to feel like I mattered, which is something that the policing process had made me doubt. I would be lying if I said that it didn't have a lasting impact on me. Whenever I see police officers now, it's hard for me to feel valued or even safe. Even with a dad who worked in the force for forty years and a brother who is actively serving.

As the proceedings concluded, I watched the driver starting to make his way out of the courtroom. He was visibly shaken from the charges that had been handed out and what they meant for his future. Still limping from the injuries that his mistake had caused me, I surprised even myself by following him outside. As we edged closer towards each other, I realised this was the first time that we had looked each other in the eye. The last time I saw this man, he had been sitting in a gutter with his head in his hands as I lay on the road going in and out of consciousness after being hit by his car.

'Are you okay?' I asked him.

He looked up at me, surprised. 'I'm not,' he said, his tears still flowing freely.

The judge and the police prosecutor had asked to have a private conversation with me, but I felt torn. I didn't want to leave this man here struggling, but I needed to respect the legal process. In the end, my dad met the judge and the prosecutor in the judge's chambers, while I stayed and talked with the man.

I'm unsure even today why I made this decision. There are perhaps unconscious reasons that I haven't yet explored, but the only thing I can put it down to is my gut feeling. I just felt a pull towards him.

'How are you getting home today?' I asked.

'I'm not actually sure,' he said.

The man's legal team had spoken about his financial hardship as part of his defence, so I knew he likely couldn't afford a taxi. And he had lost his licence so driving himself was not an option. As I looked around, I realised that, apart from his legal representatives, there was no one supporting him in the courtroom.

I looked over to Dad, who had reappeared after meeting the judge and the prosecutor. As an experienced police officer, he was no stranger to legal proceedings. His expression showed me that he knew exactly what I was about to do.

My brothers and I have a running joke that our parents have what we call 'face drop'—the expression of despair that both Mum and Dad get when one of us is in some kind of trouble. It's a mixture of despair, shock and as though they are bracing themselves for the worst possible thing to happen next.

'We'll give you a lift,' I said to the man.

It was a quiet car trip. The fifteen minutes it took felt like hours by the time we finally arrived at his address, and you could have heard a pin drop for the entire trip.

Whenever I tell people this story, they think I'm making a point about forgiveness, or they ask me if I was taking kindness to a whole new level. But neither is entirely true. I think it was more about compassion. The fact that this man had made a mistake didn't make him a lesser person. His legal defence—arguing that I was at fault—did hurt me, but it also suggested to me that he was struggling deeply with his own issues. And so, just as Erin had shown me compassion by not allowing me to suffer alone, I chose to do the same for this man, because nobody should struggle alone. And I knew from experience that kindness inspires kindness.

It takes a lot for my dad to reveal any kind of sadness or overwhelm. I have always known that my parents are proud of me, even if they haven't made a habit of explicitly telling me very often. As we sat together having lunch after our detour to the man's house, I realised for the first time just how hard it had been for Dad to watch me go through the things I had. As much as it pained me to hear what it had been like to watch me endure the things I had, I also felt tremendous gratitude towards him and Mum for being so amazingly supportive. And again, I realised that I was the lucky one in all of this. It would have been much harder to be my parents, watching me fight through so many challenges, feeling completely helpless. *That must have been torture for them*, I thought. The more my dad explained, the more I realised that I had never been alone in my suffering. The entire time I'd been grinding through rehab, they too were grinding through the effort and time that it took to support me through it all.

When I was a child I had a quote that hung above my bed that read: *The world is changed by your example, not by your opinion*. To me it was a reminder to act in accordance of who we are, rather than just talking about it. I have learned that in order for compassion to be as powerful as it can be, it must be more than its definition 'to suffer together'. The next step is almost always the most important, though it shouldn't be done out of duty, or if it's to the detriment of your own well-being. But if we can, we should ask ourselves: What can I do to relieve part of this suffering? And if there is something that can be done, do it.

That driver never once said sorry to me, or even thank you for the ride, but I hope one day he finds forgiveness for himself. Perhaps he will pay forward the kindness he was afforded when he needed it most.

• • •

Aunty Meg and I chatted long into the night, over several nightcaps. I was keen to learn about her life. She lived alone, with not even any pets. She didn't talk about her family much. I didn't want to impose, but having seen Aunty Meg spend the whole day helping others, I was worried for her.

So I asked, and Aunty Meg was open in her response, telling me she had spent time as a guest at the home we had visited that day. Her story is not mine to tell, but what I can say is that she is a wonderful example of turning adversity into something positive. I asked if I could give her a hug. I'm not sure what that moment meant to her, but it was the warmest and softest hug I have ever had. We hugged long and we hugged tight.

My bed for the night was in a downstairs guestroom— it was nothing fancy, but everything that I needed for a good night's sleep. Which is exactly what I had, as I slept uninter- rupted for the entire night, waking to Aunty Meg's footsteps at eight o'clock the next morning. As I headed out to the kitchen to enjoy the breakfast Aunty Meg had cooked for me, I was surprised to see my things at the door, neatly packed as if I had somewhere to be.

As I ate, Aunty Meg told me I had twenty minutes for a shower, then she'd take me to the airport. Out of her own pocket, she had purchased a flight to get me home so I could be with my family and friends.

I was surprised, and even a little confused, but I was ready. This was without doubt the perfect ending to my journey. Meeting Aunty Meg and sharing in the difficulties of the women to whom she had devoted herself, and being able to share my story with them, had been one of the most moving experiences of my life.

As a young adult, it baffled me how often we see hate in the world—whether in the form of bullying, domestic violence, gun violence or any other man-made adversity or suffering—and then respond to that hate with negativity, planning revenge, or even influencing others to perform acts of hatred on our behalf. Where does it stop?

What if, instead, we let that hate stop with us? What if we take a stand and respond with compassion and understanding, to halt the spread of further hatred and adversity? The world would be a better place, right?

My journey had given me so many opportunities to experience compassion in action, but none had a greater impact on me than the time I spent with Aunty Meg. The compassion she showed sent a clear message to those she helped: 'I see you, I hear you and I value you—and you are not alone.' I vowed to carry this spirit with me when I returned to my life at home.

The choice

I had travelled for just over two months, and visited so much of Australia. Incredibly, around 10,000 people had reached out to me with offers of kindness, but I'd only been able to connect with 98 of them in person. They had housed me, fed me, transported me from place to place, kept me company or simply said hello. Each exchange was unique and special. I'd had plenty of laughs, and I had cried a lot as well—in a good way, for the most part. It was overwhelming to have that many people show up for me.

Writing doesn't come naturally to me, so my decision to blog for an hour every day might seem an odd choice, and I hadn't planned to do so until the very first night, when I was staying with the Parks in Sydney. But already I knew that my journey would have a profound impact on me, and I wanted to remember as much of it as I could.

I will be forever grateful to every person I met. And to every person who liked or shared one of my social media posts to help me get the word out. To those who sent me messages, not only with offers of help but simply to wish me well; some people told me they would pray for me.

I believe I learned more about myself during that two-month journey than I have in the rest of my life so far. Travelling solo tends to do that, and the complexity of travelling on the kindness of strangers amplified the effect. I truly started to find myself, and life became beautifully brilliant again.

If I had to summarise what I learned, it's this. Human beings crave connection. We were born to connect. Those who are the happiest and healthiest among us have strong social connections.

So why do we sometimes find it so hard to connect with one another? Is it that our lives have become so technologically advanced that we've forgotten to say thank you to the person who makes our coffee, or to smile at a stranger as we pass by?

I know we can find human connection if we cultivate the building blocks of kindness: self-acceptance, perspective, humility, gratitude, mindfulness, positivity, collaboration, empathy, trust, humour, honesty and compassion.

Remarkably, after I got home to Sydney, I felt like my kindness journey had only just begun. I left my job in sports administration and began travelling the world, sharing my story as a motivational speaker. I still grapple with this as my job title, having only really learned the trade on this very journey. But the more I have come to do of it, the more I have realised that being yourself on a stage is something that most audiences are drawn to. I appeared in front of corporate audiences, on mine sites, before war veterans and even at some of the hospitals where I'd been a patient. But where I was happiest was always in front of children.

'If she can, I can'—that's the belief I hoped anyone hearing me would carry away with them. And that is my hope for you, too, as the reader of this book. I'm no more special than the next person. In my line of work, I hear from people around the world who have endured all manner of hardships. They will often reach out to me in their darkest moment and ask how I have endured the things I have. The truth is, life will never be easy—but a broken heart can still beat. When we make a choice to carry on with a heavier heart than most, we pay tribute to the memory of the loss that we have endured. Whatever that may be.

Writing this book has given me greater insight into myself. At times I surprised myself with the things I remembered. *Wow, I didn't even know that I felt that way*, I often thought. I suspect I had repressed aspects of my story because I didn't want to think about them.

About two months into my writing process, I was diagnosed with ADHD—which made a lot of sense to me, but brought a new set of challenges. When I was at primary school I was often labelled as highly distracted, and reading and comprehension were not my strong points. So to have written a book about some of the hardest moments in my life sometimes felt like herding cats. Working through all of these feelings has been a growth experience in itself. So if you're reading this, thanks for coming through this process with me.

The most common question I get asked after sharing my story is: 'How did you get through the things you did?' And that's almost always followed by: 'Why did you choose kindness as the path forward?'

Here's what I think. Everything we do in life is a choice. Every interaction we have with ourselves and with others has the potential to change the course of someone's day—to lift them up or drag them down. That is the power we hold as human beings. It is both a tremendous opportunity and a tremendous responsibility. When we appreciate this, we come to see that it is our choice whether these interactions are positive or negative. Life really can be that simple.

My hope is that this book might serve as a reminder that, even in the midst of suffering, we can still choose kindness. We can still choose to be the person we want to be—the person we would be proud to be, just like my friend Dawid.

When I was in the depths of some of my struggles, I often looked to others for inspiration, all the while knowing that, deep down, I had the resources I needed to get through every challenge. I had the power to choose a better life—for myself and for all the people who believed in me. I genuinely don't believe that I would be walking today, for instance, without the belief and support of my best friend, Erin.

The same can be said for how we choose to see our world. We can choose to see the world that mainstream media and social media often depicts, which at times seems the very opposite of kind. Or we can actively choose to tip the balance by responding with kindness. If ever I need reminding of this, I give Sergio a call.

I know and accept that I occupy a very privileged position. I have been able to access some of the best medical and psychological care in the world, and my background means I have not faced challenges which many others do. I have not overcome everything that I have because of myself alone. I have been fortunate, and it has taken a village of people to get me to where I am.

If you are struggling, please reach out to someone. A friend, a family member or a professional. I am still connected with a great psychologist, who is only ever a phone call away should I need it—she actually helped me write parts of this book. No one should go through life alone, and there is absolutely no shame in asking for help. On the contrary—it shows great strength.

If you have noticed a friend struggling, please show up for them. Do so in the hope that if you ever find yourself in a similar position, someone might do the same for you. No one goes through life without suffering. Kindness and all that we have learned it to be is, quite honestly, the greatest gift you can give.

Acknowledgements

To every person who sent me best wishes or an offer of help who I wasn't able to meet on the trip, thank you. I wasn't able to read every offer—there were simply too many—but I smiled every time my inbox lit up or I saw a message come through. At the time, as you now know, smiling wasn't such an easy thing for me to do before leaving. Thank you.

To my family. I love you all, and as difficult as it must have been to sit with me, you supported me and held your breath instead of shouting at me when I was stubborn or doing things that were outside of the box. Thank you. No family is perfect, but ours is perfect to me. When I tell people that I am the youngest of four and the only girl, with three older brothers, people often joke and say that they feel sorry for me. But I wouldn't have it any other way.

To Grant. My brother and my rock. Please don't ever change. Thank you for understanding me. And for ALWAYS showing up for me. I love you so much.

To Nan. I know you're not around to read this. But it's important for me to acknowledge the impact you had on my life. Without a doubt, you are the strongest person I have ever known. I miss having cappuccinos with you.

My Grandparents. Outside of the journey I have just written about, I learned more through watching you be you than I did in any classroom or lecture hall. Thanks for always keeping it real.

To my friends. My chosen family. Erin, Whip, Isa, Carla, Carly, Corinne, Tahnee, Clare—what a bloody ride it's been. My favourite thing about all of us is that we've never been afraid to be ourselves. In the good times and the bad. Thank you for laughing with me, even when it wasn't appropriate to do so. Thank you for always showing up and for always supporting me. It's your friends who make your world and my world is perfect because of you all.

To Mrs Bromhead. Can you believe I wrote a book?! My entire schooling journey was better because you cared about me. And whenever I speak in front of teachers now, I reiter-ate the power of caring about your students because of you. I also tell them that you failed me in almost all of my English exams—and now I'm a motivational speaker and a published author. So there's hope for all of the struggling students out there!

Debbie. I respect you so much. Thank you for your patience and for putting up with my stuff.

To Tessa from Allen & Unwin. I'd been approached four times to write a book before your email snuck itself into my inbox and we agreed to meet up. I knew then that I had a person I could trust who would help guide me through this writing process. Thanks for believing in me to tell it the way that we have—and for believing in kindness as deeply as I do. Geez, you deserve a medal for being as patient as you have been with me. Thank you so much.

I get a lot of credit for the work and impact of the Kindness Factory. But it wouldn't be anything but an idea if it weren't for one person in particular: Greg Healy, Chairperson of the Kindness Factory. It struck me during this writing process that Greg didn't feature. But this is because we began working together more closely after the journey was complete. Greg, in the past six years you've become someone I couldn't imagine my life without. I know I drive you up the wall at times. In some ways, we are like chalk and cheese—I am a dreamer and you are a planner. But in other ways, we are very similar—we both believe in decency and doing good in the world. I appreciate you more than we talk about and probably more than you know.

To the Kindness Factory board, past and present—this book wouldn't have happened without you. I feel like I've been on my last legs a few times throughout our six-year journey of existence. But every time I've felt like falling over, one of you has shown up in a way that has kept me going. Thank you for your completely voluntary service and commitment to the movement. But most importantly, thank you for your friendship.

To Kaplan and Rob Regan in particular. You were the first partner to truly get behind the Kindness Factory, and what we have been able to create together has been extraordinarily special and will impact lives well into the future.

Finally, to the people who I met on this journey. I feel that I could have written an entire book on each of our experiences alone. Thank you for letting me tell your stories. And thank you for being there for me. I had no idea what the future held before leaving, but this journey changed my life. I learned more in those two months with you than I have the rest of my entire life. I cannot thank you enough.

Resources

If you need immediate assistance, please call 000.

If you would like to talk about your situation, you may wish to contact one of the following services:

Adults:

Lifeline
Lifeline is a non-profit organisation that provides free 24-hour telephone crisis support services in Australia.
Call 13 11 14—24 hours a day, 7 days a week
lifeline.org.au

13YARN

13YARN is a free and confidential national crisis support helpline run by and for Aboriginal and Torres Strait Islander people, providing a culturally safe space for mob who are feeling overwhelmed to yarn about any needs or concerns and explore options for on-going support.

Call: 13 92 76—24 hours a day, 7 days a week

13yarn.org.au

Suicide Call Back Service

Suicide Call Back Service provides free counselling for suicide prevention and mental health via telephone, online chat and video chat for anyone affected by suicidal thoughts.

Call: 1300 659 467—24 hours a day, 7 days a week

suicidecallbackservice.org.au

1800RESPECT

1800 RESPECT is the national online and telephone counselling and support service for people who have experienced, or are at risk of experiencing, sexual assault and/or domestic and family violence, or their family and friends, and for isolated frontline workers.

Call: 1800 737 732—24 hours a day, 7 days a week

1800respect.org.au

MensLine Australia

Mensline Australia offers free professional telephone counselling support for men with concerns about mental health, anger management, family violence (perpetuating and experiencing), addiction, relationships, stress and wellbeing.

Call: 1300 78 99 78—24 hours a day, 7 days a week

mensline.org.au

Beyond Blue

Beyond Blue provides information and support to help everyone in Australia achieve their best possible mental health.

Call: 1300 22 4636—24 hours a day, 7 days a week

beyondblue.org.au

Youth

Kids Helpline

Kids Helpline is a 24-hour telephone service that is available for young people (aged between 5–25) who need advice, counselling or just someone to talk to—no problem is too big or small.

Call: 1800 55 1800—24 hours a day, 7 days a week

kidshelpline.com.au

ReachOut

ReachOut offers online tools designed with—and specifically for—young people. It is 100% online, anonymous and confidential, allowing young people to connect on their terms: how they want to, when they want to. ReachOut offers a wide range of support options including one-to-one peer support, moderated online communities, tips, stories and resources. au.reachout.com

Other resources:

Kindness Factory (acts of kindness log): kindnessfactory.com
The Kindness Curriculum (school and home resources): thekindnesscurriculum.com
Gotcha4life (building mental fitness): gotcha4life.org